Brand Atlas

Alina Wheeler
and Joel Katz

Brand Atlas

Branding intelligence made visible

WILEY

John Wiley & Sons, Inc.

For general information about our other products and services, please contact our Customer Care Department within the United States at (800) 762-2974, outside the United States at (317) 572-3993 or fax (317) 572-4002.

Wiley also publishes its books in a variety of electronic formats. Some content that appears in print may not be available in electronic books. For more information about Wiley products, visit our website at www.wiley.com.

Library of Congress Cataloging-in-Publication Data

Wheeler, Alina, 1948– author.
Katz, Joel, 1943– author.
  Brand Atlas : Branding Intelligence Made Visible / Alina Wheeler, Joel Katz.
      p. cm
  Includes index.
    ISBN 978-0-470-43342-3 (hardback)
1. Brand name products. 2. Branding (Marketing) 3. Trademarks- Design. I. Title.
  HD69.B7W43 2011
  658.8'27–dc22
                                        2010049604
Printed in the United States of America

10 9 8 7 6 5 4 3 2 1

BRAND ATLAS

Who are you?

Who needs to know?

Why should they care?

How will they find out?

Contents

1 Dynamics 10
Brand Landscape

Global Sourcing	12
Speed	14
Design Thinking	16
Word of Mouth	18
Conversation	20
Interconnected	22
Open Source	24
Social Networks	26
Experience	28
Passion	30
Transparency	32
The Cloud	34
Sustainability	36
Mobility	38
Crowdsourcing	40
Free	42
Placemaking	44
Choice	46

2 Intelligence 48
Brand Basics

Brand as Identity	50
Vision	52
Needs and Desire	54
Touchpoints	56
Purpose	58
Spirit and Soul	60
Perception	62
Authenticity	64
Positioning	66
Stakeholders	68
Big Idea	70
Brand as Asset	72
Brand Extensions	74
Brand Alignment	76
Brand Architecture	78
Recognition	80
Trademarks	82
Names	84
Good and Different	86

3 **Drive**   84
Brand Management

Branding	90
Simplicity	92
Culture	94
Collaboration	96
Time Management	98
80/20	100
Competencies	102
Insight	104
Focus	106
Customer Service	108
Customer-centric	110
Growth	112
Metrics	114
Fight or Flight	116
Onliness Exercise	118
Perceptual Mapping	120
SWOT Exercise	122
Flow	124

4 Details   126

Brand Questions	128
Project Management	130
Brand Decisions	131
Branding Process	132
Big Idea Process	133
Bibliography	134
Credits	137
Index	138
Gratitude	141
Authors' Reflections	142
Diagram Matrix	143
About the Authors	144

Why *Brand Atlas*?

The first modern world atlas was created in 1570. Gerardus Mercator inspired Abraham Ortelius to create a navigation tool for seafaring traders. It was called *Theatrum Orbis Terrarum*, or *Theatre of the Round World*. Their collaboration rendered a user-friendly innovation that was based on a simple idea: a compendium of maps to help people understand where they are in relationship to where they need to go.

In this spirit, *Brand Atlas* makes it easier to understand and navigate the brand landscape. Global competition is fierce. Consumers are inundated with choices.

The velocity of change is both exhilarating and challenging. New platforms and technologies distract brand managers from essential brand fundamentals. The team is racing to create the brand of choice, to build trust, and to be irreplaceable.

Brand is an organization's most valuable asset. Brand managers must manage this intangible asset to achieve tangible results. They want to embrace the dynamics of the marketplace while staying true to the fundamentals of branding. They seek the right tools and the best thinking in their organizations.

Brand Atlas has a structure that reflects the three critical competencies for building a sustainable brand: insight into marketplace dynamics and trends, an understanding of brand basics, and access to the best processes, tools, and exercises.

Brand Atlas has three objectives: brevity, synthesis, and clarity.

Brevity. Distilling the relevant ideas and imperatives of brand thinking to their essence; utilizing provocative diagrams to illuminate concepts, processes, and tools; recognizing that people learn in different ways.

Synthesis. Capturing the best thinking and best practices of brand building from thought leaders and practitioners; integrating brand fundamentals with marketplace dynamics.

Clarity. Demystifying branding with straightforward simplicity; providing access to the most incisive thinking; synthesizing word and image to convey the salient aspects of branding.

Brands have become the global currency of success. Emerging markets, corporations, communities and individuals are leveraging their brands to gain a transcendent advantage in the marketplace. Positioning a brand to be irreplaceable is the new business imperative for both public and private sectors, regardless of the product or service.

Alina Wheeler
Joel Katz

Global Sourcing 12

Speed 14

Design Thinking 16

Word of Mouth 18

Conversation 20

Interconnected 22

Open Source 24

Social Networks 26

Experience 28

Passion 30

Transparency 32

The Cloud 34

Sustainability 36

Mobility 38

Crowdsourcing 40

Free 42

Placemaking 44

Choice 46

1
Dynamics

Brand Landscape

Your product, service, platform, or app is fighting for shelf space, media coverage, and visibility, for the opportunity to prove that it is the one that your customer will notice, try, and love. While brand principles are durable, the dynamics change daily. Section 1 reveals how marketing dynamics can be harnessed to jumpstart the branding process. It delineates how social networking, open source, apps, freeconomics, and other platforms can be the building blocks for introducing, extending, and sustaining your brand.

11

Global Sourcing

Brands, capital, goods, and services flow ceaselessly around the globe. Fashion, technology, and tools are designed here, made there, and sent everywhere. Business services are outsourced to the Czech Republic. Code is written in Brazil. Leading global brands are choosing to be transparent about the origin of their raw materials, the location of their factories, their environmental footprint and their labor practices. Patagonia customers log on to The Footprint Chronicles to track a product's origins. Nissan's car stickers delineate the source country of the car's components.

Design a global strategy to take advantage of market opportunities and production economies. Respect cultural differences and cultivate political awareness. Pay attention to the bottom line, but not at the expense of your customer.

You can ride knowing that your purchase was not a vote for deforestation, for poor labor practices abroad, for excessive materials transportation and fossil fuel consumption.
Comet Skateboards

Which is the more American product, a Honda Accord built by Ohioans for a company with its headquarters in Japan, or a Ford Fusion built in Mexico for a corporation that is based in Michigan?
Cheryl Jensen
The New York Times

The practice of conscious capitalism can show that profit and prosperity go hand in hand with social justice and environmental stewardship.
Dr. Shubhro Sen
Co-founder
The Conscious Capitalism Institute

13

Speed

The indefatigable pace of innovation renders the business landscape always new and unfamiliar. Platforms, models, and values like open source and the free economy are radically altering the terrain. This momentum is symbolized by Moore's Law, Gordon Moore's prediction that the number of transistors per square inch on integrated circuits would double every two years. Consumers are poised to keep up to the velocity of profound technological change. Can brands afford to lag behind? It is essential for organizations to embrace networks and systems that are transforming the way customers make choices.

Be ready to incorporate emerging technology into your strategy. Free budgets from legacy systems so new platforms have the resources to succeed.

You have to run faster in order to stay in the same place.
   Paul Romer

There is certainly no end to creativity.
   Gordon Moore
   Co-founder
   Intel

You blink your eyes for one nanosecond and three new updates, tools, widgets, platforms and browsers have made their debut.
   Genevieve Jooste
   Social-media strategist

Technologists are all in a race to beat Moore's Law. What? Eighteen months?
   Blake Deutsch

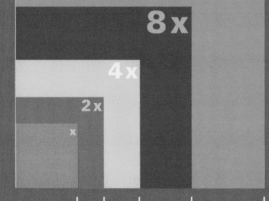

64x

32x

16x

8x

4x

2x

x

15

0   +2 yrs +4 yrs   +6 yrs   +8 yrs   +10 yrs   +12 yrs

Design Thinking

Innovation means survival for countries, communities, and consumer brands. Emerging markets are racing for the lead position in a global marketplace, while armies of algorithms stand ready to complete any task. Design thinking is an emerging methodology used by forward-thinking businesses to achieve radical, sustainable innovation in products and services. The process is powered by a deep understanding of user needs, desires, and perceptions. A cross-disciplinary team utilizes creative thinking, observation, rapid prototyping, and a nonlinear process to achieve business results.

Experiment with new ways of working and thinking. Design solutions rather than products. Merge beauty with functionality and community. Bring together left-brain and right-brain competencies.

What's in greatest demand today isn't just analysis but synthesis—seeing the big picture and crossing boundaries, and being able to combine disparate pieces into an arresting new whole.

Daniel Pink
A Whole New Mind

We are on the cusp of a design revolution in business, and as a result, today's business people don't need to understand designers better, they need to become designers.

Roger Martin
Dean, Rotman School of Management
University of Toronto

If you want to think outside the box, you've got to be outside the box.

Robin Chase
Founder
ZipCar

The biggest hurdle to innovation is the corporate longing for certainty.

Marty Neumeier
The Designful Company

CORPUS CALLOSUM

17

Left brain	Right brain
Logical	Random
Sequential	Intuitive
Rational	Holistic
Analytical	Synthesizing
Objective	Subjective
Looks at parts	Looks at whole

Word of Mouth

Elusive, uncontrollable, powerful word of mouth is the most trusted way to learn about a brand. The customer may also be a parent, a spouse, a business owner, a volunteer in her community, a blogger, a voter, or a member of a book group. She talks, emails, blogs, tweets, and posts to her Facebook page, where her posts are repeated on the pages of her 460 friends worldwide. She brags about the brands she loves and complains when brands let her down. And when she talks, her network listens.

Give your customers something to talk about. Provide an accessible way for customers to express themselves. Remember that a satisfied customer is a powerful asset.

Talking about yourself won't make others talk about you. It's about the passion conversation, not the product conversation.

Brains on Fire: Igniting Powerful, Sustainable Word of Mouth Movements

Ninety percent of word of mouth happens offline. There's a huge likelihood for word to spread about experiences people have through the service.

Brains on Fire

Trust must be the cornerstone of any word of mouth movement. You are no longer the big bad brand controlling the conversation.

Brains on Fire

19

Conversation

Before social networks changed the relationship, brand conversation was one-way, flowing from company to consumer. The monologue is now a dialogue. The consumer is no longer a faceless statistic in a report; she has become an active participant in the brand building process. Share, tag, and comment are her new mantras. The company's role is to listen and reciprocate. To be authentic, companies must respond with a human voice, not a packaged message. While brands are more vulnerable, the conversation is more dynamic and compelling and the customer is more intimately involved.

Post to social networks and blogs, which offer opportunities for more personal communications with consumers and stakeholders. Enjoy the interchange and stimulate new dialogues. Be spontaneous, relevant, and open.

We have to open up our lives to this. Ford is learning to be part of the conversation. Just by interacting with people, we've tapped into their curiosity. It's changing the way we think.

Sam De La Garza
Brand Manager
Ford Fiesta

The big revolution that's brewing is that we, the people, are sick of being numbers. We want to be seen and heard, and treated as individuals.

Chris Brogan
President
Human Business Works

The consumer voice has been amplified and the conversation has shifted beyond the traditional gatekeepers of brand managers and marketers.

Brendán Murphy
Senior Partner
Lippincott

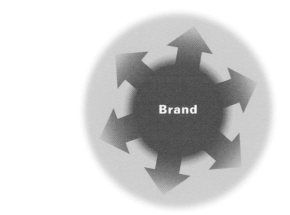

THEN

NOW

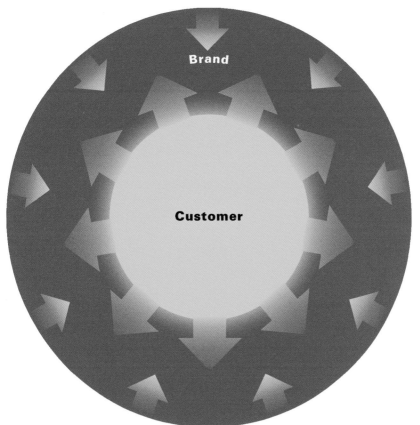

Interconnected

Our communities have become global as well as local, virtual as well as physical. Community ties, cultural identity, and strong beliefs about sustainability favor local brands, while economies of scale, choice, and speed to market favor global brands. Anyone with a big idea, a smartphone, and an app can now connect with a worldwide market and build a brand. Regardless, location should matter. It is vital that brands maintain their promises, adapt products to local needs and cultures, and take the long view on building communities and living in an interconnected world.

Understand the local needs and desires of your customers. Respect the local culture and adapt your products and services to add value.

The world is flat in a fairly general (Google) and occasionally branded (drink Coke) way. Local reality matters profoundly—ask GM in India or anyone trying to do business in Japan or China.

Dr. Gregory P. Shea
Professor
The Wharton School of the
University of Pennsylvania

If you can localize your apps, your products, you will penetrate rich diverse global markets.

Tyler White
App Developer
Flickr Photo Map for iPhone

Local brands have the home-field advantage, provided they qualify as strong brands in their own right.

Nigel Hollis
The Global Brand

Open Source

Open Source is community-generated innovation that leverages the talents of passionate users who contribute their expertise to a meaningful venture. It is a model of collaboration, creativity, and problem solving that challenges the traditional belief in creator ownership in favor of open sharing between creator and user, merchant and customer, employee and volunteer. Linux was one of the first widely accepted platforms built by communities working together in the open for mutual benefit. Originally used for software, open source is now used in product development and innovation in the public and private sectors.

Are you willing to trade predictability for possibility? Explore what happens when you apply open source principles to advance your brand innovation.

Open source is a meritocracy. Everyone has access to the same information, and the best ideas win.

opensource.com

Red Hat has utilized the power of open source as not just a software development model, but as a business and organizational model.

Jim Whitehurst
President and CEO
Red Hat

Wikipedia represents the most powerful new business model of the 21st century: open source.

Daniel Pink
Drive

SHARED USER COMMUNITY
Entrepreneur–Volunteer–For profit–Nonprofit

SHARED DEVELOPMENT PROCESS

CREATOR COMMUNITY
Entrepreneur–Volunteer–For Profit–Nonprofit

PROBLEM

Social Networks

Free form and evolving, social networks create new groups constantly around issues, events, and preferences. Online communities inspire members to post their profiles, broadcast their opinions, share their photos and videos, and connect with both friends and ideas. Brands that embrace social networking can tune in to their customers intimately, listening to the undercurrents, discovering unmet needs, identifying new markets, engaging new customers, building trust, and creating messages that resonate.

Create a dynamic and immediate communications strategy to leverage the opportunities that social networks offer.

Simply trust yourself and be who you are all the time.
Chris Brogan and
Julien Smith
Trust Agents

Social media is word of mouth on steroids.
Margie Gorman

The number of Facebook's monthly active users exceeds the population of the European Union.
Blake Deutch

YOU

Experience

Memorable experiences engage consumers and transcend products and services to create indelible impressions of the brand. The Geek Squad turns mundane computer repair into heroic encounters of a theatrical kind. American Girl Place brings American Girl dolls to life, combining education, entertainment, and retailing in a setting designed to appeal to girls and their moms. The most compelling experiences combine all realms of engagement: entertainment, educational, escapism, and esthetic. A compelling experience generates positive buzz and new ways to generate income.

Consider what might make your offerings more fun and provide a better sense of escape. What could customers learn from exploring new activities? What would make customers want to just hang out and be with you and your brand?

Goods and services are no longer enough.

B. Joseph Pine II and
James H. Gilmore
The Experience Economy

The American Girl Place is the epitome of the branded experience; it has a strong philosophy, clear values, and a founder/visionary who wanted to create the experience of a lifetime for her customers.

Nancye Green
Principal
Donovan/Green

Yes we're geeks, but we won't talk over your head. When we work with you, we'll walk you through the process so that you can do the little things to keep your technology running smoothly.

geeksquad.com

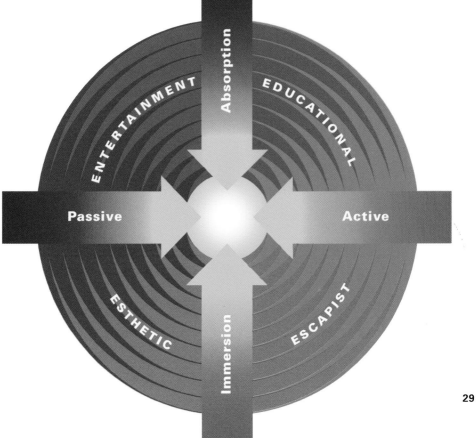

Passion

Embracing technology, a single passionate individual can inform, inspire, connect, and create. Social entrepreneurs and game changers are no longer bridled by legacy infrastructure, investments, and outmoded ways of thinking. Innovators and brand builders are forming global tribes, tapping into the wisdom of the crowd and open source collaboration. The leader's strong personal brand has the power to forge a community of individuals with a common interest, transcending nationality, gender, and ethnicity.

Start small. Think big. Stay open to all of the possibilities and follow your passion.

Passion is a multiplier of human effort, but it can't be manufactured. It's present only when people get the chance to work on what they truly care about.

Management Innovation eXchange (MIX)

The secret of leadership is simple: Do what you believe in. Paint a picture of the future. Go there. People will follow.

Seth Godin
Tribes

Everyone is a leader. Growth happens. Whenever it does, allow it to emerge. Learn to follow when it makes sense. Let anyone lead.

Bruce Mau
Chief Creative Officer
Bruce Mau Design

LEADER

IDEA

Transparency

Transparency is the new privacy. Consumers can access product information, labor practices, and environmental compliance in a few keystrokes. Bloggers reviewing products hold nothing back. Word of mouth can break as well as make a brand. Social networking is immediate and provides platforms to respond quickly and honestly. Traditionally, damage control involved the suppression of information, but those days are over. Companies who need to recover from a crisis must be open, sharing as much detail as possible.

Develop a company-wide approach to community and customer response. Create a crisis communication plan and train top executives and spokespersons in risk management.

It takes 20 years to build a reputation and five minutes to ruin it. If you think about that, you'll do things differently.
Warren Buffett

The reputation economy creates an incentive to be *more* open, not less. Since Internet commentary is inescapable, the only way to influence it is to be part of it.
Clive Thompson
Wired

By giving people the power to share, we're making the world more transparent.
Mark Zuckerberg
Co-founder
Facebook

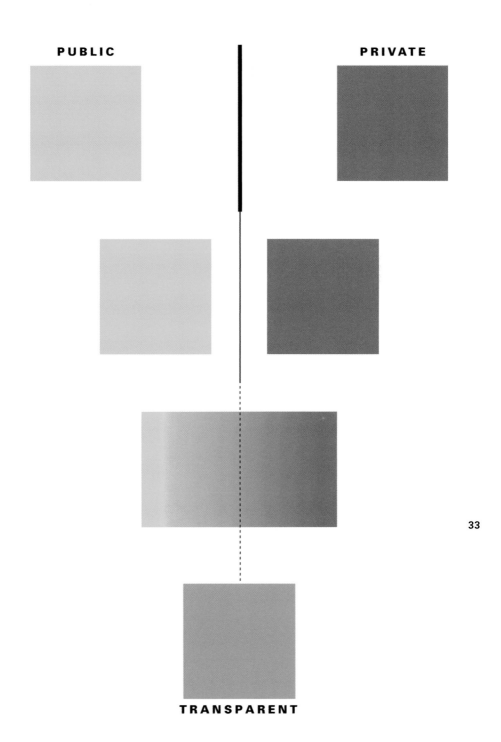

PUBLIC

PRIVATE

TRANSPARENT

33

The Cloud

Cloud computing is shifting IT applications from computers to the web, where they are shared by employees at the home office, the field force in Tokyo, engineers in Abu Dhabi, and consultants in São Paulo. The whole team can retrieve vital brand resources anywhere, accessing documents and collaborating easily. For brands, which depend on consistency, agility, responsiveness, and seamless communication, cloud computing means that messages, processes and tools can be transmitted instantly, and globally, reaching team members via their mobile devices or computers.

Select a platform that fits your needs for collaboration, project management, or analytics.

34

The move to the cloud, where applications and information are hosted on remote servers rather than privately owned computers and databases, is the latest paradigm shift in computing.

IBM Smarter Planet

Imagine

Aggregate

Collaborate

Schedule

ANYWHERE

EVERYWHERE

Sustainability

Making a difference has become integral to building brands. Consumers are shopping their values, and businesses are rethinking their social responsibility, their value proposition, their product life cycles, and their environments. The triple bottom line—people, planet, profit—is a business model that represents a fundamental shift in how businesses measure success. A new generation of social entrepreneurs believes that business can be a positive force for social change.

How can your organization make a difference? How does your leadership measure success? What values are important to your customers?

Businesses acting as businesses, not as charitable givers, are arguably the most powerful force for addressing the issues facing our society.

Michael Porter
Bishop William Lawrence
University Professor
Harvard Business School

With every pair you purchase, TOMS will give a pair of new shoes to a child in need.

TOMS Shoes

We're open to manufacturing product anywhere as long as they meet our criteria for human rights and safety and everything else.

Bert Jacobs
Co-founder
Life is good

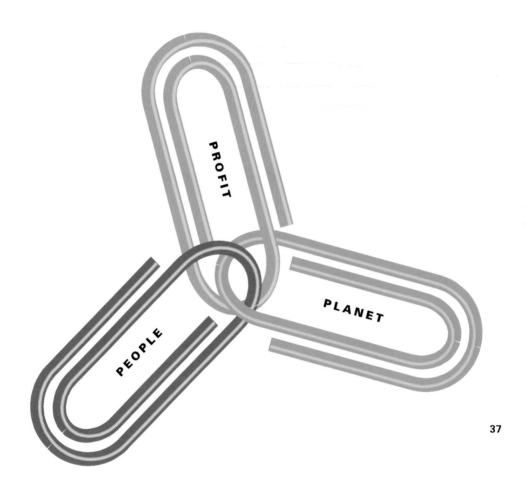

Mobility

The iPhone, iPad, Droid, and other mobile devices have freed users from their desktops, allowing people to communicate, conduct business, post, play games, shop, and follow their friends. Employees will be soon be going to their company app stores to get sanctioned applications that can be customized for their own work environment. Location-based apps help retailers communicate with nearby customers, and shopping apps allow chains to constantly market new products. Apps have become the new collectible for consumers, and every brand needs them.

Does your brand have an app? Has your website been optimized for mobile devices? Is your company ready to use mobile apps in the workplace?

By 2015, Forrester Research predicts that half of all devices on US corporate networks will be mobile.
Bloomberg Businessweek

Whirlwind is IBM's online storefront for employees, offering apps for everything from approving purchase orders to scheduling meeting rooms.
Bloomberg Businessweek

Mobile is the new online, online is the new offline! That means mobile is the new ad network, the new data substrate, the new product screen, the new shopping list.
Paul Kedrosky
Infectious Greed blog

39

Crowdsourcing

Big consumer brands use crowdsourcing
as a way to engage their audience in brand
building, inspiring customers to make a video,
create a slogan, or design something cool
in exchange for a moment of media glory.
Nonprofits issue an open call on the web
in hopes of generating original marketing.
User-generated content is evolving into user-
generated creativity. Crowdsourcing accesses
the collaborative culture of the web to attract
and motivate consumers. Honesty, clarity, and
carefully communicated expectations and outcomes are necessary.

*Determine whether crowdsourcing will help
you attract more customers, gain marketing
insights, or dilute your brand positioning.
Ensure that the PR and brand management
functions are in sync.*

In open source, everyone
who contributes benefits.
Crowdsourcing may have many
contributors but fewer benefi-
ciaries.

Chris Grams
President and Partner
New Kind

Crowdsourcing is the act of
taking a job traditionally per-
formed by a designated agent
(usually an employee) and
outsourcing it to an undefined,
generally large group of people
in the form of an open call.

Jeff Howe
Crowdsourcing

If creativity is the gift of a
talented few, why are so many
people suddenly creative?

Patricia Martin
Tipping the Culture

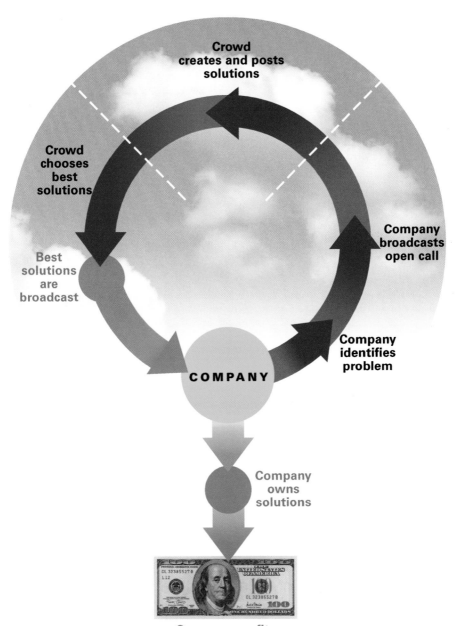

Crowd
creates and posts
solutions

Crowd
chooses
best
solutions

Company
broadcasts
open call

Best
solutions
are
broadcast

COMPANY

Company
identifies
problem

Company
owns
solutions

Company profits

Free

Freeconomics is one of the biggest challenges facing traditional businesses, like newspapers, who have learned that sooner or later you will compete with free. It drives the huge profits of digital companies like Google and jump starts bands like Radiohead. It may mean redesigning the relationship between the company and its audience and redefining the market. When radio started broadcasting—for free!—the same questions about monetization arose. Can free be profitable? Yes, but finding the right formula can be a challenge.

Be intentional and strategic about what you offer for free. One way free makes money is by making other things more valuable, like free iPhone apps that charge for expanded features.

The truth is that zero is one market and any other price is another. In many cases, that's the difference between a great market and none at all.

Chris Anderson
Free: The Future of a Radical Price

Once a marketing gimmick, free has emerged as a full-fledged economy.

Chris Anderson
Wired

Who doesn't love freebies in life?

The Fring app

43

✗ Placemaking

Placemaking, a new brand competency, creates experiences for consumers across an array of venues, offering encounters so engaging and true to the brand that they spark loyalty and word of mouth. Visiting an Apple store is like stepping inside an iPad. Similarly, LEGO's portfolio of Legolands, Imagination Centers, Mindstorm experiences inside science museums, and its User Group Network let customers directly experience the brand. Brands must prove they are what they say they are in intentionally designed places, both physical and virtual.

Consider what portfolio of experiences, from singular flagships to those ubiquitously accessible worldwide or on the web, would best create demand for your offerings.

Starr Tincup Needs to focus on Placemaking.

The experience is the marketing. A brand is the promise of an experience.
James H. Gilmore and **B. Joseph Pine II**
Authenticity

Provide a place for customers to understand, use, play with, and fundamentally experience your offerings in a place and time that demonstrates that you are what you say you are.
James H. Gilmore and **B. Joseph Pine II**
Authenticity

SINGULAR
PLACE

Flagship
location

Flagship
site

Experience
hubs

Experience
domains

Major
venues

Major
platforms

Derivative
presence

Derivative
placement

World wide
markets

World wide
web

45

UBIQUITY

PHYSICAL
ACCESS

VIRTUAL
ACCESS

Choice

Today's consumer is accustomed to a precise
level of choice in product selection. A family of
three may routinely purchase creamy peanut
butter for their son, crunchy for Dad, and salt-
free for Mom. Teens may insist on an iPhone,
college students request an iPad, while their
parents are happy with a Droid. A product with
distinct features, pricing, or service will attract
its own audience. The vital brand challenge is
to dramatically tell each product's story so the
appeal reaches the market.

*Make it easy for your customers to
discern between the choices you've
provided. Brainstorm different choices
to attract new customers and consider
opportunities to customize.*

The expansion of choice
has become an explosion
of choice, and while there
is something beautiful and
immensely satisfying about
having all of this variety at our
fingertips, we also find our-
selves beset by it.

Sheena S. Iyengar
The Art of Choosing

Mass customization is effi-
ciently serving customers
uniquely. Customers are
markets of one—everyone is
unique and deserves to get
exactly what they want at a
price that they are willing to
pay.

B. Joseph Pine II
Co-founder
Strategic Horizons LLP

CHOICE OF PRICE / QUALITY

CHOICE OF STYLE

Brand as Identity 50

Vision 52

Needs and Desire 54

Touchpoints 56

Purpose 58

Spirit and Soul 60

Perception 62

Authenticity 64

Positioning 66

Stakeholders 68

Big Idea 70

Brand as Asset 72

Brand Extensions 74

Brand Alignment 76

Brand Architecture 78

Recognition 80

Trademarks 82

Names 84

Good and Different 86

48

2
Intelligence

Brand Basics

The landscape changes daily: Brand principles provide the central, underlying strategy for successfully reaching your customers, creating motivation and desire. As you shape your big idea, identify your appeal, articulate your positioning, and create your brand identity, your brand acquires resonance and meaning. A successful brand is an asset whose value transcends tangibles like real estate and technology. It is created by you, but it resides in the hearts and minds of loyal consumers who choose you.

49

Brand as Identity

Branding has become the singular most important activity for a business, an organization,
or an entrepreneur. When feudal domains
became economic enterprises, the battle for
territory evolved into competition for share of
mind. The need to brand emerges from fundamental questions about identity: Who are you?
Who needs to know? Why should they care?
How will they find out?

*Answer these questions quickly: Who are
you? Who needs to know? Why should they
care? How will they find out? You have begun
the branding process.*

[handwritten: Purpose, brand market, value prop, marketing strategy]

Brands help consumers cut
through the proliferation of
choices available in every
product and service category.
Scott M. Davis
Brand Asset Management

How could I have been anyone
other than me?
Dave Matthews
Dave Matthews Band

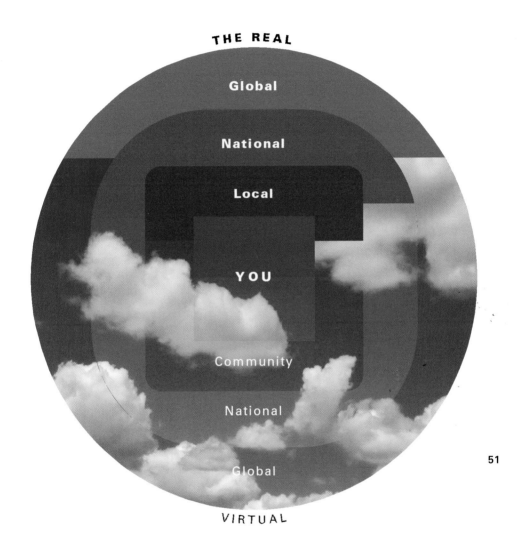

THE REAL

Global

National

Local

YOU

Community

National

Global

VIRTUAL

51

Vision

Vision requires courage. Big ideas, enterprises, products, and services are sustained by individuals who have the ability to imagine what others cannot see and the tenacity to deliver what they believe is possible. Brands often begin with a dream to make the world a better, easier, happier place. For mature organizations, it's important to revisit the vision, its meaning, and relevance. The process can galvanize the brand's contribution, motivating and inspiring new initiatives as well as everyday operations. A vision that aligns values, unites communities of interest, and carries the company in good times and in crisis.

Is your vision statement accessible and relevant today? Can it sustain your organization through rapidly changing times?

eBay pioneers communities built on commerce, sustained by trust, and inspired by opportunity.
eBay mission

We believe we can end poverty and injustice, as part of a global movement for change.
Oxfam vision

Google's aim is to organize the world's information and make it universally accessible and useful.
Google vision

Wow, wouldn't it be great to create some symbol that represents optimism.
Bert Jacobs
Co-founder
Life is good

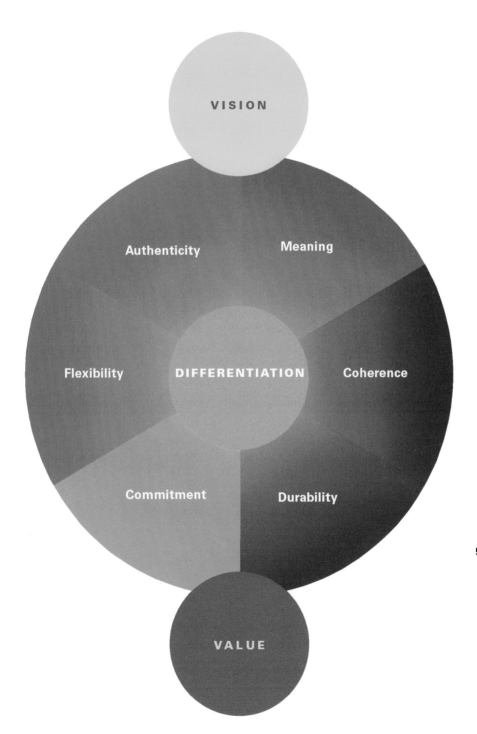

VISION

Authenticity

Meaning

Flexibility

DIFFERENTIATION

Coherence

Commitment

Durability

VALUE

53

Needs and Desire

Brands that recognize the role of desire can position their products and communications to address primary human needs. We all want to be safe and secure, loved and respected, attractive and creative, connected to our families and communities. Psychologist Abraham Maslow's hierarchy of needs reveals that needs, like instincts, motivate human behavior. Within each customer is a desire to actualize the potential for love, achievement, recognition, and belonging.

Remember that the emotional connection of your brand transcends its features and benefits. The best brands satisfy more than one need, fulfilling higher desires at the same time.

Maslow's Hierarchy of Needs:

Self-Actualization
Creativity
Flow
Problem Solving

Esteem
Confidence
Achievement
Respect

Love, Belonging
Friendship
Intimacy
Community

Security
Safety
Resources
Family
Health

Survival
Breathing
Food
Water
Balance
Sleep
Sex

The job is not to find the right customers for your products but to find the right product for your customers.

Philip Kotler
Marketing Management

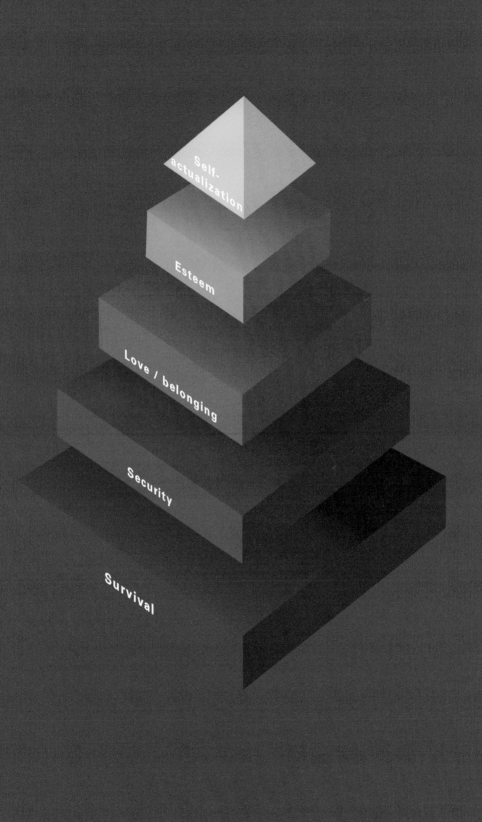

Touchpoints

We can see it, hear it, experience it. The best brand touchpoints fuel recognition, amplify differentiation, and arouse emotions. Each touchpoint is an opportunity to extend loyalty, attract a new customer, or inspire a blogger to write an enthusiastic post. A touchpoint can be as large as a retail environment, as ephemeral as an email, as complex as a user manual, and as small as a business card. Touchpoints should create desire, spark perception, and embody a brand's essence.

Conduct an internal and competitive audit. Compare your touchpoints and the competition's. Determine whether your brand is cohesive across channels.

Industry - Brand Touchpoints.
Record the general voicemail.
Look @ the business cards
Ask for everything

Having a centralized brand center accessible through the web ensures that our teams—whether in Paris, Hong Kong, or Mumbai—have access to our brand guidelines and full library of marketing materials.

Gail Galuppo
Chief Marketing Officer
Western Union

The brand exists in a dynamic sales and marketing matrix.

Blake Deutsch

While look is defined by color, scale, proportion and motion, feel is experiential and emotional.

Abbott Miller
Partner
Pentagram

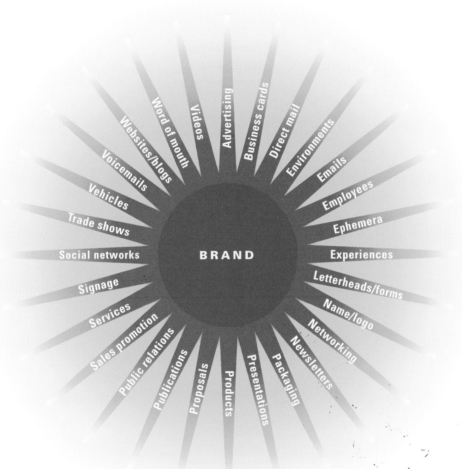

BRAND

Word of mouth · Videos · Advertising · Business cards · Direct mail · Environments · Emails · Employees · Ephemera · Experiences · Letterheads/forms · Name/logo · Networking · Newsletters · Packaging · Presentations · Products · Proposals · Publications · Public relations · Sales promotion · Services · Signage · Social networks · Trade shows · Vehicles · Voicemails · Websites/blogs

Purpose

Brands who do one thing better than anyone else and deliver on their promises are unstoppable. In *Good to Great*, Jim Collins demonstrates how growth and greatness spring from companies that have a purpose beyond profit, strong core values, and a disciplined culture. His hedgehog model has three imperatives: "Determine what you can be best in the world at. Determine what drives your economic engine. And determine what you are deeply passionate about." Any organization, regardless of size or sector, can benefit from thoughtfully responding to these imperatives.

What is your purpose beyond making money? Is there a single thing that you do better than anyone else? Do your customers, employees, and stakeholders know?

A hedgehog concept is not a goal to be the best. It is an understanding of what you can be the best at.
Jim Collins
Good to Great

Imagine a world in which every single person on the planet is given free access to the sum of all human knowledge. That's what we're doing.
Jimmy Wales
Co-founder
Wikipedia

What are you passionate about?

PASSION

What drives your economic engine?

PROFIT

PURPOSE

What can you be best in the world at?

59

Spirit and Soul

How does a brand reach consumers' hearts and minds? David Aaker's Brand Identity Planning Model examines the ways brands appeal to their audience. A **symbol** has the power to evoke a spectrum of feelings and associations and the potential to become a familiar suggestion. A brand that focuses on a **person** can convey a relationship and a layered, multi-faceted personality. Brand as **organization** can embody trust, innovation, values, and community involvement. A brand organized around a quintessential **product** can communicate functionality and quality. Each is emblematic in its own way.

How does your brand reach and appeal to consumers? What feelings and associations do you want customers and prospects to have when they experience your brand?

Branding adds spirit and a soul to what would otherwise be a robotic, automated, generic, price-value proposition.

David Aaker
Vice Chairman
Prophet
Building Strong Brands

A business has to be involving, it has to be fun, and it has to exercise your creative instincts.

Sir Richard Branson
Founder and CEO
Virgin

BRAND AS PERSON

BRAND AS SYMBOL

BRAND AS PRODUCT

BRAND AS ORGANIZATION

61

Perception

Brands connect to the mind and the heart. Brand identity is tangible and appeals to the senses. Consumers want brands that understand them. Emotions and perceptions drive their choices. Color, sound, feeling, and experience design are used to evoke emotions and express personality. Smartphones have become objects of desire, and many brands are chosen for what they say or don't say about the consumer. In a multicultural society, brands need to demonstrate that they respect and understand cultural differences.

Research why customers select your brand. Investigate the layers of competitive advantage that are subtle, emotional, and perceptual. Use design and experience to connect emotionally with your customers.

In a world that is bewildering in terms of competitive clamour, in which rational choice has almost become impossible, brands represent clarity, reassurance, consistency, status, membership—everything that enables human beings to help define themselves. Brands represent identity.

Wally Olins
On Brand

Keep the higher level promise of your brand and your name, logo and core colors, as visible and consistent as possible.

Connie Birdsall
Creative Director
Lippincott

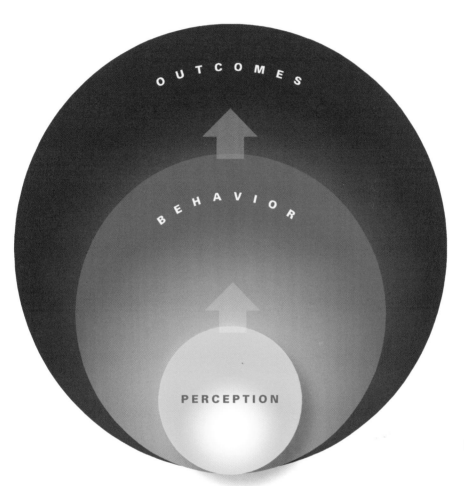

Authenticity

Consumers are drawn to brands that they perceive are original, engaging, and responsive—that live up to their promise and their vision, values, culture, and personality. Their authenticity protects and sustains them. Organizations who know who they are and what they stand for start any brand-building task from a position of strength. To build authenticity, agree on brand essence and apply it to every trademark, tagline, key message, and interaction. A brand is not a logo, but a logo should unlock positive associations and strengths.

Does your organization have a shared understanding of what your brand stands for and the value that it provides? Authenticity is knowing who you are.

Authenticity, for me, is doing what you promise, not "being who you are."
Seth Godin

As reality is qualified, altered, and commercialized, consumers respond to what is engaging, personal, memorable, and above all, authentic.
James H. Gilmore and **B. Joseph Pine II**
Authenticity

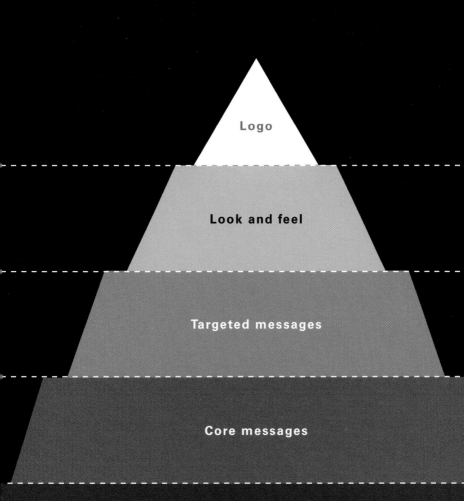

Logo

Look and feel

Targeted messages

Core messages

We know who we are

Positioning

Insight into the perceptions of the customer is the driving force behind all marketing efforts. Al Ries and Jack Trout's groundbreaking work revealed that every product must be positioned in the customer's mind, rather than described with countless features. It is essential to determine the brand's target audience, price, distribution, and key messages. Does it embody cutting-edge innovation or classic values? Does it appeal to status seekers or bargain hunters? Is it differentiated from the competition? All channels should reflect those decisions, from the logo to packaging, distribution, apps, and the website.

Research! The more you know about your target customer's needs and desires, your competition, and the needs you fill, the more effective your message and the more loyal your audience.

A brand becomes stronger when you narrow its focus.
Al Ries and **Jack Trout**
The 22 Immutable Laws of Branding

While the timeless positioning principles endure, the methods brands use to effectively establish their positioning must change drastically.
Chris Grams
President and Partner
New Kind

Positioning is the most important skill in marketing, Product, service, initiative, or idea—if you don't actively position it, someone else will do it for you.
Sterling Brands

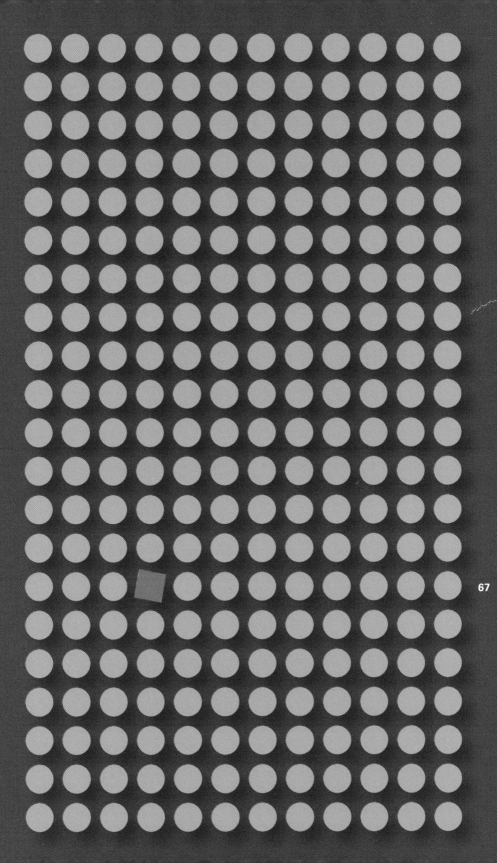

Stakeholders

Stakeholders are the constituents who affect the success of a brand. Reputation and goodwill extend far beyond a brand's target customer. Employees, contractors, community organizations, suppliers, shareholders, and members of the media can be advocates, influential champions promoting and supporting the vision. Transparency, attentiveness, and a policy of quick response to all stakeholders will support branding goals. Research about stakeholders will inform a broad range of solutions from positioning to the tilt of brand messages, the launch strategy, and plan.

Recognize the importance of having all stakeholders on your side. Let them know you are listening and acting on their concerns.

B Corporations are for sustainable business what LEED is for green buildings. It's about the business as a whole—how they treat their employees, how they're engaged in their local community, how they treat their suppliers, and how they are good stewards of the environment.

Jay Coen Gilbert
Founder
B Corporations

A company's reputation is established through the implicit and explicit promises that it makes to a variety of communities, be they investors, customers, suppliers, employees, regulators, or the media.

Elizabeth Lux
The Wall Street Journal

You live or die by your database.

Chris Brogan and **Julien Smith**
Trust Agents

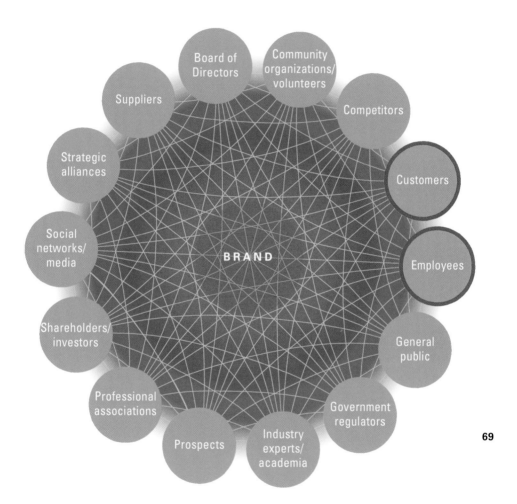

Big Idea

The big idea is the scaffolding that supports brand strategy, behavior, actions, and communications. It is the essence of the brand and its core purpose. A big idea is articulated by the company and recognized by the consumer as the reason the brand is chosen, cherished, and enduring. A smarter planet is IBM's big unifying idea, adding vitality to life is Unilever's. Just do it. Think different. Big ideas provide a competitive advantage and help top managers stay laser-focused as they invent new products and services, reduce their portfolio of sub-brands, and recruit employees.

Is your big idea sufficiently articulated to guide marketing, expansion, and divestiture? Does it dramatically differentiate you from your competitors? Are you making it easy for your customer to choose your brand?

For GE, imagination at work is more than a slogan or a tagline. It is a reason for being.

Jeff Immelt
Chairman and CEO
GE

Building a better world is not so much a goal as an everyday fact of life.

Brian Walker
CEO
Herman Miller

Park Angels is a movement of people coming together in the name of their public spaces.

Robbin Phillips
Courageous President
Brains on Fire

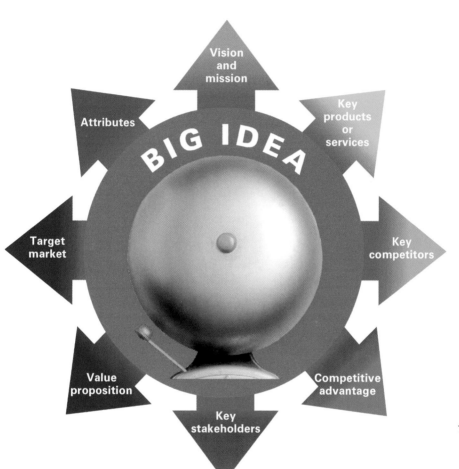

Brand as Asset

For most businesses, brands represent their most important and valuable asset, since they influence customer choices, investors, and employees. Numerous studies by respected management consultancies have substantiated that the average brand accounts for more than one-third of shareholder value. Many brands are identifying strategies to increase their portfolio of intangible assets and decrease their tangible assets. Increasingly, large nonprofits have begun to utilize brand valuation data to support fund development. Methodologies to determine valuation are not universal.

Which part of your business is most valuable? Have you trademarked your brand assets? What actions are you taking to protect and grow your brand assets?

When most key financial indicators plummeted, the value of the top 100 brands rose by four percent in the last year to more than $2 trillion.
Millward Brown

Companies use brand value as a tool to obtain financing, put a price on licensing deals, evaluate mergers and acquisitions, assess damages in litigation cases, and justify the price of their stock.
Marty Neumeier
The Brand Gap

In 2010, the brand value of Coca-Cola was valued at 63 percent of market cap; Google was valued at 83 percent of market cap.
Blake Deutsch

BRAND
VALUE

Brand Extensions

Changing technology and new global markets set the stage for new products, services, and shopping venues. Brand extensions—new products that are spin-offs of an existing brand —can extend its reach, leverage new opportunities in the market, or attract a new audience with a similar product. There are economies of scale to be realized in the production, marketing, and distribution of related products and services. While success will strengthen the brand, the risk is that failure will undermine the parent brand.

Carefully evaluate brand opportunities to avoid diluting or damaging the core brand. Look for opportunities to build equity.

Test fast, fail fast, adjust fast.
Tom Peters

Every company needs to understand what its brand does and does not stand for before it tries to extend it in an uncharted direction that may not fit with the needs of the marketplace.
Scott M. Davis
Chief Growth Officer
Prophet

You can't just ask customers what they want and then try to give that to them. By the time you get it built, they'll want something new.
Steve Jobs
CEO
Apple

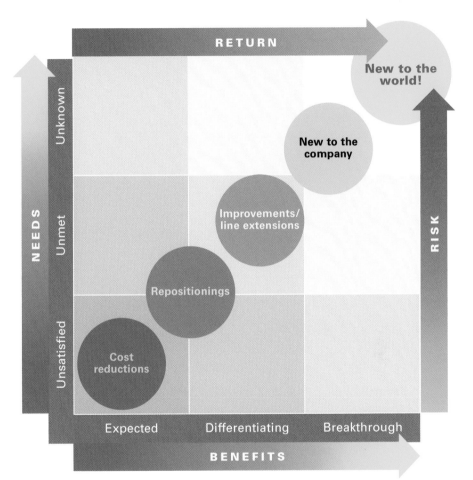

75

Brand Alignment

Every time customers experience a brand, it should feel familiar. Whether they are using a product, talking to a service rep, or making a purchase from their iPhone, the contact should feel cohesive. Alignment begins internally with adherence to a dynamic central idea. It extends to the actions of all employees. It is communicated with a distinctive voice, look and feel, and it culminates with the experience of customers, whether they are in Buffalo, Beijing, or Timbuktu, in a store, on the phone, or online.

How do you do promote immediate recognition of your brand? Are brand attributes visible across marketing channels and media?

Unify. Simplify. Amplify.
Ken Carbone
Co-founder
Carbone Smolan

Organizations, people, and projects need to build greater alignment and integration between who they are, what they say, and what they do.
Michael Hogan
Principal
Brandology

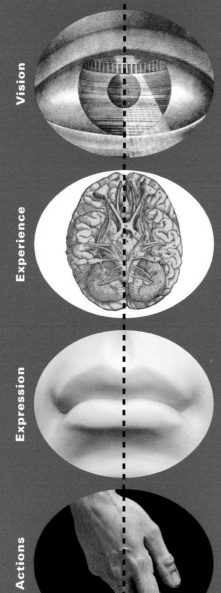

ALIGNMENT

Vision

Experience

Expression

Actions

ALIGNMENT

77

Brand Architecture

Smart naming, flexible brand architecture, and a unified verbal and visual system facilitate the marketing of any new product or service. Brand architecture refers to the hierarchy of brands within a single organization, and communicates the interrelationship of the parent company, its subsidiaries, products, and services. There are three major categories: **Monolithic** architecture is characterized by a strong, single master brand. **Endorsed** products or subsidiaries benefit from a strong association with their parent. In the **branded** strategy, the name of the holding company is frequently invisible to the consumer.

Determine which strategy mirrors your marketing structure and goals. Anticipate how to best build your business and your brands. As you acquire new brands, be clear about the brand architecture strategy before you sign on the dotted line.

Each brand architecture model has advantages and disadvantages. To make a decision, look at the marketplace, identify potential gaps in the market, assess in detail the brand portfolio, the company ambition, the core idea and weigh the pros and cons of each choice.
Wally Olins
The Brand Book

Most organizations start with one name, one identity, and one brand. However as businesses grow they make acquisitions, and these acquisitions may in turn own several companies or brands, and they then need to decide what to do with the names they have acquired.
Wally Olins
The Brand Book

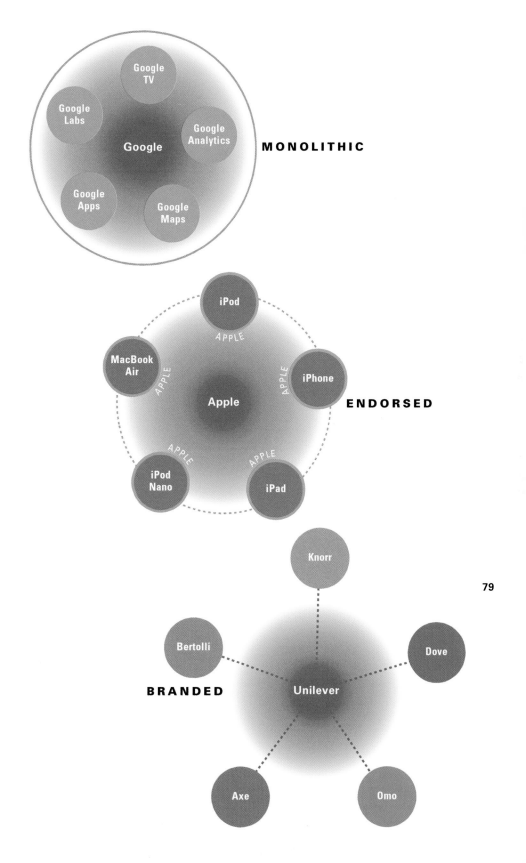

MONOLITHIC

ENDORSED

BRANDED

Recognition

The way the brain processes symbols gives us insight into the speed of brand recognition and how logos function when there is frequent exposure. Visual identity triggers perceptions and unlocks associations of the brand. Sight, more than any other sense, provides information about the world. The brain acknowledges shapes first, followed by an emotional connection to color. Third and last, the brain reads text and understands language. This explains why customers recall a brand when they see part of its distinctive shape.

Does your logo use distinctive shapes to make it memorable? Calculate how many times a year your logo is seen across marketing channels.

Logos are the fastest form of communication known to man.
Blake Deutsch

The logo is the gateway to the brand.
Milton Glaser
Designer

You can recognize a consumer brand by just seeing part of a shape.
Heidi Cody
Cultural Anthropologist

Letterforms from:
Budweiser
Reese's
Adobe
Netflix
Disney

81

Trademarks

The best logos convey a big idea or brand attribute, embody strategic positioning, and differentiate from the competition. From literal to symbolic, from word-driven to image-driven, recognition is fueled by frequency and consistency. Design is the integration of meaning and form. Although some meaning is perceived initially, the full meaning emerges and is nurtured over time. Excellence evolves from a thoughtful design process that examines both aspirational and functional criteria.

Create a clear set of usage guidelines for your logo, for both internal and external partners. In a redesign, determine whether the change is evolutionary or revolutionary.

This new evolution of our logo embraces and respects our heritage. At the same time, it evolves us to the point where we feel it is more suitable for the future.

Howard Schultz
Chairman and CEO
Starbucks

Design differentiates and embodies the intangibles—emotion, content and essence.

Moira Cullen
Global Design
The Hershey Company

Brand names:
Google
Starbucks
Bayn
Univision
Nike

Wordmark

A freestanding acronym, company name, or product name that has been designed to convey a brand attribute or positioning

Pictorial mark

An immediately recognizable literal image that has been simplified and stylized

Emblem

A mark in which the company name is inextricably connected to a pictorial element

Letterform

A unique design using one or more letterforms that act as a mnemonic device for a company name

83

Abstract/symbolic mark

A symbol that conveys a big idea, and often embodies strategic ambiguity

Names

Distinctive, meaningful, and memorable
names are a brand asset. Customers can
easily search and find them. They stand out
from the competition, work visually in logo-
types and in text, and seamlessly apply to
brand extensions. They position their brands
for growth, change, and success. Finding a
name that can be legally protected and offers
a viable URL is a formidable challenge. The
team wants to fall in love with the name
immediately and commit to it. Meaning and
associations, however, are built over time and
use.

*Use brainstorming techniques to generate
hundreds of options. Record all ideas.
Examine names in context. Write stakeholder
quotes and say them out loud.*

Don't pick a name that makes
you one of the trees in the
forest and then spend the
rest of your marketing budget
trying to stand out.
  Danny Altman
  Founder
  A Hundred Monkeys

Naming is 20 percent creative
and 80 percent political.
  Danny Altman
  Founder
  A Hundred Monkeys

Just by naming a process, a
level of service, or a new service feature, you are creating a
valuable asset that can add to
the worth of your business.
  James Bitetto
  Partner
  Tutunjian & Bitetto, PC

Founder

Easy to trademark. Satisfies an ego. Poses a challenge when the person retires.

Fabricated

Easier to trademark. Requires a larger investment to educate the market.

Descriptive

Conveys the nature of the business. Challenge is diversification.

Metaphor

Great for storytelling possibilities. Has built-in latitude.

Acronym

Difficult to remember and difficult to trademark. Requires a huge investment in advertising.

Magic spell

A distinctive spelling must be easy to say. Works best when the name has meaning.

Good and Different

Brand history is filled with value-creating ideas that were quickly rejected by customers in focus groups who said they would never buy it. Leading the list are brands like Post-it Notes, Cirque du Soleil, and Herman Miller's Aeron chair. The riskiest ideas (i.e., good and different) are often the ones that have the potential for lasting profits. Innovation never tests well. Marty Neumeier's Good and Different tool gives many companies the courage to green-light an innovation.

What would it take for your organization to have a radically differentiated brand? If your brand didn't exist, would anyone notice? Be irreplaceable.

Business success today comes from converting imagination, empathy, and collaboration into patents, brands, and tribes.
Marty Neumeier
Director of Transformation
Liquid Agency

We want to make Google the third half of your brain.
Sergey Brin
Co-founder
Google

When everyone zigs, zag.
Marty Neumeier
ZAG

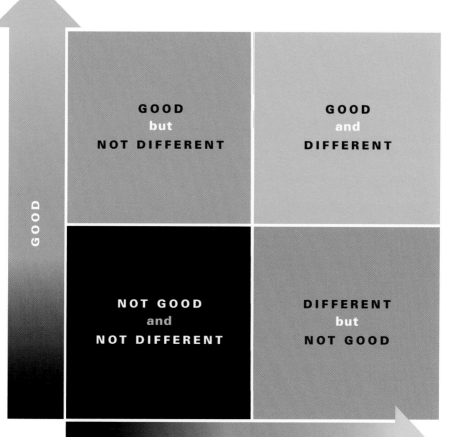

87

Branding 90

Simplicity 92

Culture 94

Collaboration 96

Time Management 98

80/20 100

Competencies 102

Insight 104

Focus 106

Customer Service 108

Customer-centric 110

Growth 112

Metrics 114

Fight or Flight 116

Onliness Exercise 118

Perceptual Mapping 120

SWOT Exercise 122

Flow 124

88

3
Drive

Brand Management

Your brand must flourish in a landscape that changes daily. It needs to be resilient, flexible, memorable, and appealing. How can your team shape and sustain this valuable asset so that it works and keeps on working? Today there are a range of tools, tactics, exercises, and approaches to support creativity, direction, and the essential choices involved in brand building. Section 3 gives you an insight into how these approaches create a synchronicity that sustains the brand process.

Branding

The branding process requires investigation, strategic imagination, design excellence, and project management skills. Patience and an ability to synthesize vast amounts of information and insights are required. Regardless of the complexity of the engagement, the process remains the same. What changes is the depth with which each phase is conducted, the length of time, the resources allocated, and the size of the team. A disciplined process facilitates decision making and signals that a proven method is being used to achieve business results.

Trust the process. The most sustainable creative work begins with agreement on the brand brief. Managing assets, the most difficult phase, has the biggest return.

Work with talented people to create something that will be of compelling benefit to the customer.

Susan Avarde
Managing Director
Global Branding, Citi

The client is the author. We are the interpreter.

Bart Crosby
Crosby Associates

Navigating through the political process—building trust—building relationships—it's everything.

Paula Scher
Partner
Pentagram

Please see page 132 for an indepth list of the process steps.

5
Manage
assets

4
Create
touchpoints

3
Design
identity

2
Clarify
strategy

1
Conduct
research

Simplicity

In a multitasking, multimedia, multimessage world, simplicity seems counterintuitive. But in branding, it is essential. To resonate and reach any audience with a compelling idea, message, or logo, teams must strive for simplicity. The appeal of text messages and Twitter's 140-character limit exemplify consumers' longing for the most streamlined communication. Simple design always trumps complexity. Repetition and familiarity are memorable and comforting.

Resist complexity. Take the time to reduce meaning to its essence, regardless of the medium. Realize that your customers are reassured by repetition and recognition.

Identify every barrier that keeps people away from your offerings, especially for first-time customers. Then systematically tackle each one, using a combination of simplicity, clear communication, and customer-centered design.

Tom Kelley
Founder
IDEO

A great brand is based on a simple idea that is unique and relevant. Simple trumps everything.

Allen P. Adamson and **Martin Sorell**
BrandSimple

Almost all quality improvement comes via simplification of design, manufacturing... layout, processes, and procedures.

Tom Peters

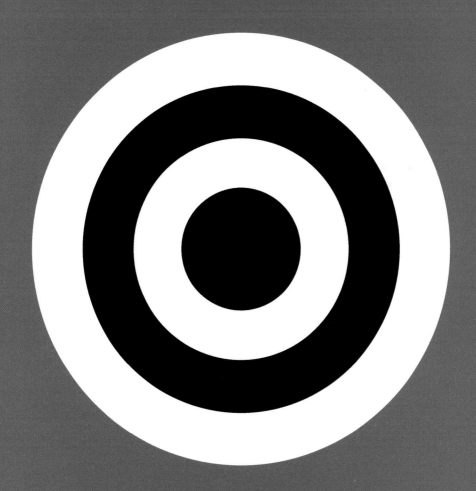

93

Culture

Long-term success is directly influenced by the way employees share in their company's culture—its values, stories, symbols and heroes. Building the brand from the inside out means inspiring employees to embrace the purpose of the organization and to commit to the values of the culture. A culture that encourages individual difference and free expression is more likely to produce new ideas and products that engage customers.

Does your culture promote listening and the free exchange of ideas? Are your employees brand champions?

Is who we say we are reflected in the way we act towards each other and our customers? It's time to initiate culture change when an organization's results are no longer supported by its behavior.

Hanley Brite
Principal and Founder
Authentic Connections

I view my role more as trying to set up an environment where the personalities, creativity and individuality of all the different employees come out and can shine.

Tony Hsieh
CEO
Zappos.com

Culture is the set of shared attitudes, values, goals, and practices that characterizes an institution or organization.

Merriam-Webster's 11th Collegiate Dictionary

Hierarchy and chain of command	Network of reliable relationships
Official values and vision	Experienced values and vision
Written rules, policies and procedures	Unwritten rules and social norms
Business contracts (internal and external)	Informal contracts (internal and external)
Business accountabilities	Social accountabilities
Information/communication systems	The back channel and rumor mill

Collaboration

Great outcomes require vision, commitment, and collaboration. Collaboration is not consensus or compromise. It evolves from a thoughtful and genuine focus on problem solving, generating an interdependent, connected approach. It also acknowledges the tension between different viewpoints and different disciplines. The brand is the common purpose that unites a company across departments and diverse agendas. Centralized, user-friendly guidelines build brand engagement and make it easy for the whole team to build the brand one touchpoint at a time.

Unleash the power of collaboration inside your organization to build your brand, and then with your customers and colleagues to innovate.

Like King Arthur's Round Table, effective teams acknowledge and respect diverse expertise, share power, actively debate, unite around a common purpose, and use their collective intelligence to achieve ambitious goals.

Moira Cullen
Global Design
The Hershey Company

We win in science, business, and life when we discover the power of collaboration. And when we work together with colleagues from near and far to push the limits of knowledge and possibilities.

Alan S. Gregerman
President and Chief
Innovation Officer
Venture Works

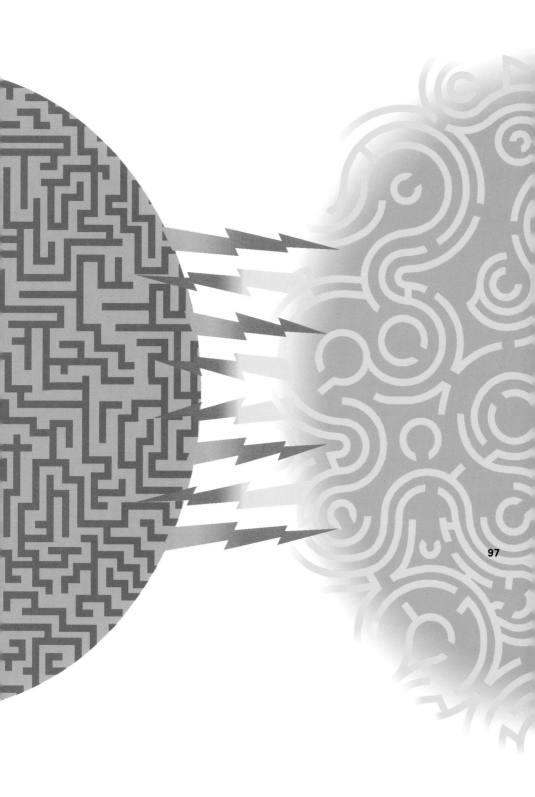

Time Management

Brand building is vital to an organization. Time management is the ability to separate the vital from the trivial. Making it easy for employees to be brand champions is an investment with a high return. Brand management has been transformed by user-friendly guides, tools, and templates that are available online all the time. These tools support strategic marketing, consistent communication, and quality execution, and save time, money, and resources. Most importantly, it keeps the whole organization focused on the meaning of the brand.

Develop brand standards to save time, money, and resources. Make the guidelines available to all employees and all external brand agencies.

Do what is important for the long term. Important trumps urgent.
Stephen Covey
First Things First

The key question to keep asking is, "Are you spending your time on the right things?" Because time is all you have.
Randy Pausch
The Last Lecture

Companies like IBM and Dell, are instituting "quiet time," when all electronic devices need to be turned off. Who knew?
Blake Deutsch

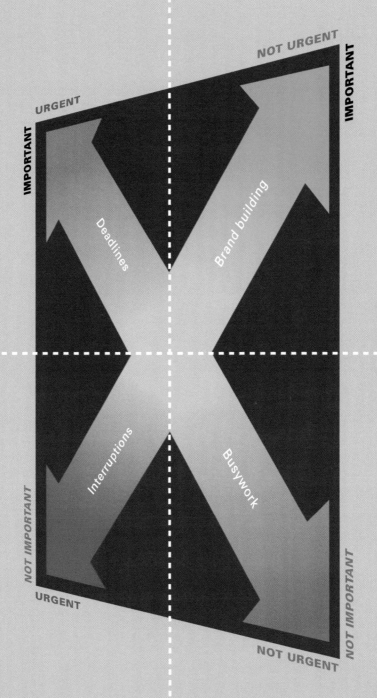

IMPORTANT

URGENT

NOT URGENT

IMPORTANT

Deadlines

Brand building

NOT IMPORTANT

URGENT

Interruptions

Busywork

NOT IMPORTANT

NOT URGENT

99

80/20

The 80/20 rule, originally known as the Pareto Principle, reveals that 80 percent of results come from 20 percent of causes. It has become shorthand in the business world for getting teams to focus on the tasks that matter most, brands that are the most profitable, and the customers that are centers of influence. Applying the rule shows that 80 percent of outcomes come from 20 percent of effort and time, 80 percent of revenue comes from 20 percent of products, 20 percent of the sales force produces 80 percent of profits.

Identify the 20 percent that matters most. Pay attention to the 20 percent of your product line that really sells, and the 20 percent of customers who spend the most.

Think global, act local is still applicable. Consider the 80/20 rule: 80 percent the same, 20 percent designed for local cultural customs, materials, economic dynamics.

Connie Birdsall
Creative Director
Lippincott

Apply your energies more effectively, looking for the payoffs that provide a multiplier of reward. Few things really matter. They matter a great deal.

Richard Koch
The 80/20 Principle

What? 90 percent of tweets come from 20 percent of tweeters?

Blake Deutsch

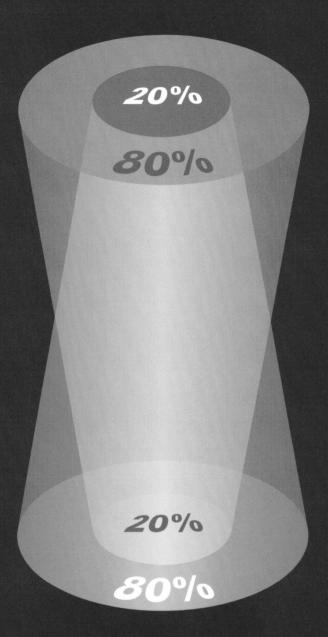

Competencies

What was the marketing department is now the branding team, and the CEO is engaged. The team now includes vital new members: the directors of design, user-experience, and social media. The basic disciplines to build an unstoppable brand remain the same: strategy, creativity, analytics, and execution. The basics of brand management remain the same: understand and listen to the customer, investigate the competition, discern emerging trends, and seize every opportunity to be the brand of choice. The biggest challenge is staying focused on the brand.

Take the branding team off-site. Rethink your priorities and processes. Research best practices and brainstorm.

What strategic choices have you made about how to compete and win? What role can marketing investment play in supporting these outcomes?
Michael Dunn
Chairman and CEO
Prophet

The aim of marketing is to know and understand the customer so well that the product or service fits him and sells itself.
Peter Drucker
Management consultant

Strategy

Analytics

Execution

Creativity

Insight

The insights, opinions, and feedback of customers can be the catalyst for change and lead to breakthrough products and compelling new customer experiences. Listen and build your brand around a deep understanding of customers' lives and how your product and interactions work for them. Tap into data analytics, survey tools, and competitive information. Consumer brands are mining social networks, following passionate bloggers who offer unedited feedback on unmet needs. Brands that understand their customers are more likely to forge lifelong, loyal relationships.

Find ways to see the world through the eyes and experiences of your customers. Take the time to make brand insights understandable to your team.

Not everything that counts can be counted, and not everything that can be counted counts.
Albert Einstein

Answering questions is relatively easy. Asking the right question is more difficult.
Michael Cronan
Co-founder
Cronan

WISDOM

Learning

KNOWLEDGE

Thinking

information

Distillation

Focus

No one does it alone. Revitalizing an existing brand or developing a strategy for a new brand requires strategic imagination and methodical examination. The desired outcome can usually be described in a sentence, but distilling the learnings from interviews, research, and audits takes skill and patience. Analysis and discovery go hand in hand. The best consultants facilitate the process by asking the right questions, providing relevant input and ideas, getting key issues to surface, and achieving resolution.

Set expectations for the investment of time necessary to conduct research and clarify strategy. Find ways to engage your organization and build trust in your process.

In a world of information overload and lack of trust in major institutions, the power of a simple idea conveyed through branding is more important than ever.

Richard Edelman
President and CEO
Edelman Worldwide

Organizations today can speak poetically—whether through written voice, visual brand, or the culture and passion of their people.

Jonathan Opp
Director of Poetics
New Kind

Please see page 133 for an in-depth list of research and strategy steps.

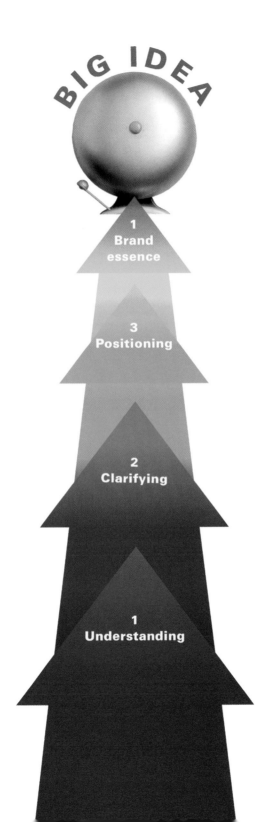

BIG IDEA

1
Brand
essence

3
Positioning

2
Clarifying

1
Understanding

Customer Service

Customer service is about balancing the intuitive and the intentional. Historically, call center reps had scripts and a limit to the time they could spend with a customer. This rigid system did not build trust, customer relationships, the brand, or the business. Companies like Zappos have revolutionized customer service. Employees work without scripts, quotas, or time limits. New employees spend four weeks as customer service reps during their orientation.

Keep the focus in customer service on the customer. Be open to challenges, innovation, and change.

Zappos Family Core Values

1   Deliver WOW through service
2   Embrace and drive change
3   Create fun and a little weirdness
4   Be adventurous, creative, and open-minded
5   Pursue growth and learning
6   Build open and honest relationships with communication
7   Build a positive team and family spirit
8   Do more with less
9   Be passionate and determined
10 Be humble

Business/company driven
Prescribed
Rigid
Managed
Scripted
Managing costs

Service/relationship driven
Intuitive
Flexible
Trusting
Unscripted
Building loyalty

CUSTOMER SERVICE GAUGE

109

Customer-centric

It takes an entire company working in concert to serve and support the customer during different aspects of the relationship. The point of sale is one of many opportunities to build trust and to extend the customer relationship. It's vital that all teams, from IT to customer support, focus on being customer-centric, which means seeing the world through the eyes of the customer. Companies that take the time to ensure that all employees understand what the brand stands for are more likely to collaborate to ensure that the promise to the customer is delivered.

Collaborate with colleagues in operations, customer service, IT, and sales to provide customers with a positive and seamless brand experience.

Given the intensity and richness of customer interactions, there are multiple avenues for differentiating the brand as experienced by customers that go well beyond the product itself.

Mohanbir Sawhney
Kellogg on Branding

Never let your business processes dictate your customer's experience.

Mike Wittenstein
Experience Designer

Even the most mundane transactions can be turned into memorable experiences.

B. Joseph Pine II and **James H. Gilmore**
The Experience Economy

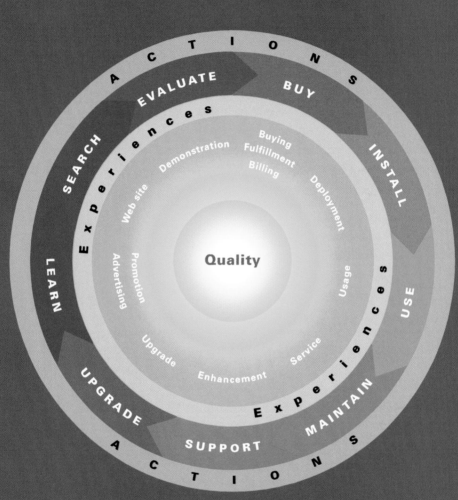

111

Growth

Each time a marketing expenditure is made, it needs to stimulate customer loyalty and new demand. Each dollar spent on marketing must inspire at least one of five consumer behaviors. Growth is driven by customers who 1) try the product, 2) pay more for a brand than others in the category, 3) increase the percentage of their budget spent on the product, 4) remain a loyal customer, and 5) recommend the company. Investing in the long term health and equity of a brand feeds short term revenue-generation activities.

Identify the steps and resources needed to go from your current performance to your vision of success.

Marketing spending can create value by generating short-term revenue and building long-term brand value. Real marketing accountability is about improving returns, not simply measuring them.
Michael Dunn
Chairman and CEO
Prophet

Spending more on marketing will not make a flawed product or service more desirable. At the same time, no successful product is so great that it cannot be derailed by poorly conceived or executed marketing.
Michael Dunn
Chairman and CEO
Prophet

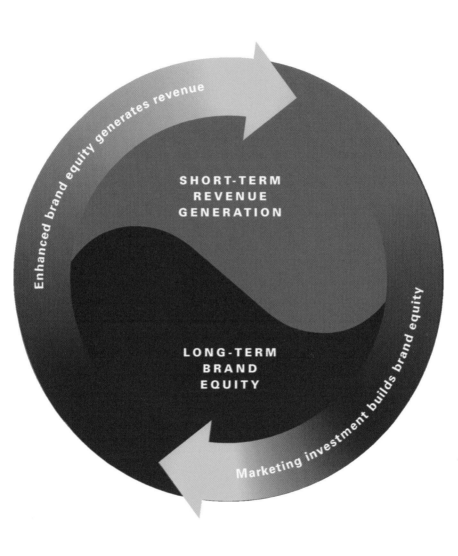

113

Metrics

Examining the gap between existing and potential performance helps leadership teams define strategic priorities, evaluate resources, guide decisions, and determine steps to be taken. What is your vision of success and what metrics do you utilize to inform continuous improvement? It is also critical to examine other brands in the same industry. Can you identify any metrics from best practice leaders? Mind the gap: Benchmark where you are and where you want to be.

Decide on specific metrics that you are going to measure. Use unbiased data to inform planning and strategies for continuous improvement.

You need to establish metrics to be able to accurately measure performance.
Heidi Caldwell
Brand Consultant

First say to yourself what you would be; and then do what you have to do.
Epictetus

You get what you measure.
Blake Deutsch

MARKET SHARE

Where you want to be

THE GAP

Where you are

TIME

115

Fight or Flight

Each branding initiative begins with euphoric optimism. Everything is in place: The CEO supports the investment, the team leader sets priorities, and a branding firm is retained. But inescapably, there is a crisis, an unforeseen barrier to reaching the goal. Even when the team has the knowledge, experience, and wisdom to deliver the results, there is a breakdown in the process. Some call it the fight or flight moment because it becomes the defining moment. Teams who work through this inevitable barrier become stronger.

Keep the goal in sight and focus on the big picture. Expect the process to encounter barriers and setbacks. Support all team members when the interaction is most difficult.

The ability to handle life's ongoing cycle is an indicator of one's ability to prosper at even higher levels to accomplish our aspirations.

Dan Calista
CEO
Vynamic

Through a shared understanding of what obstacles stand in the way, teams can develop a smarter process and more meaningful outcomes.

Dr. Ginny Vanderslice
President
Praxis Consulting Group

Once we worked through our crisis of meaning in our project, a sense of informed optimism helped us achieve completion.

Blake Deutsch

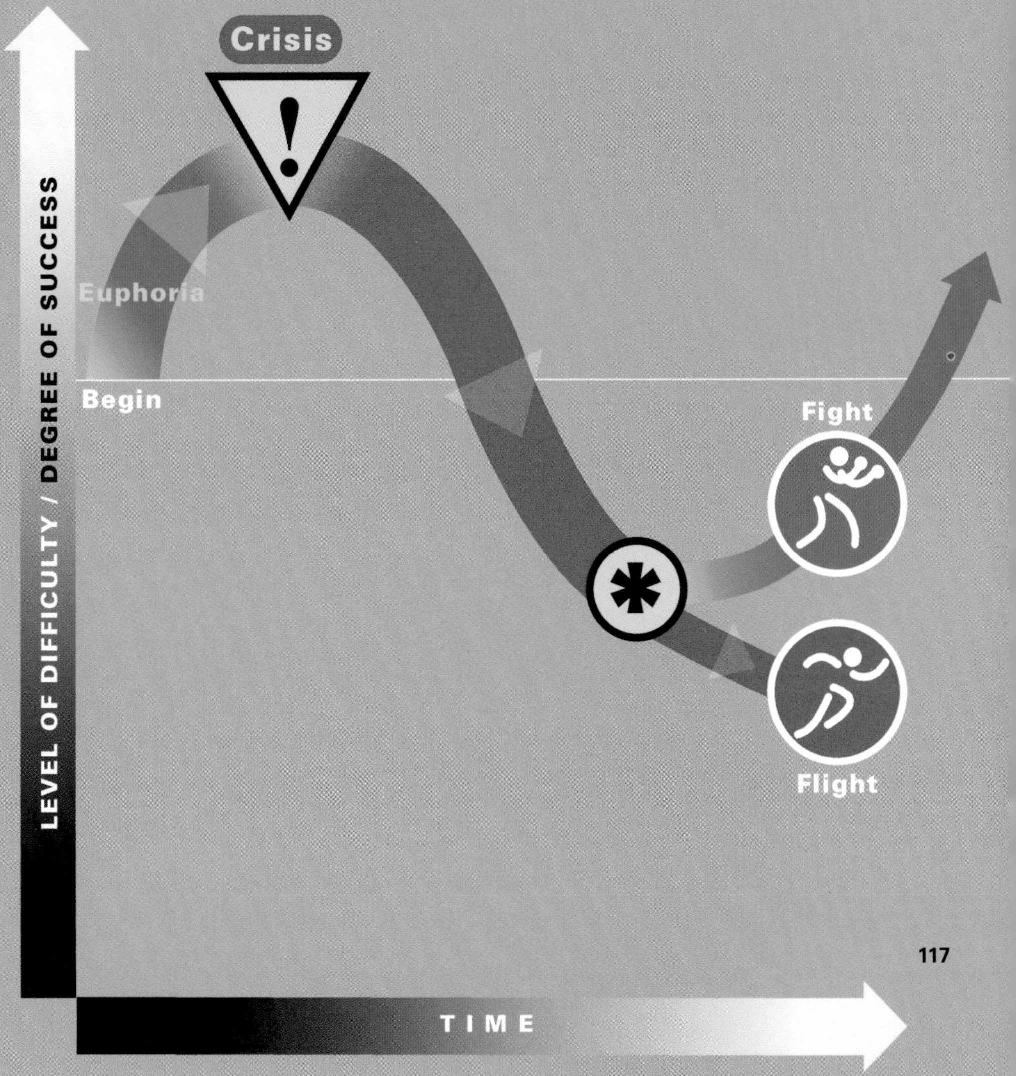
Crisis
Euphoria
Begin
Fight
Flight
LEVEL OF DIFFICULTY / DEGREE OF SUCCESS
TIME

Onliness Exercise

Cirque du Soleil is the only circus that does not have animals. Staking claim to be the "only" brand, product, or service that is radically different amplifies a formidable competitive advantage. Volvo was the first car brand with a safety value proposition. Harley Davidson was the only motorcycle brand that built on rider passion to create an evangelistic fervor for millions of customers. Marty Neumeier believes that if a company can't say briefly state what differentiates its brand from the competition, the team needs to go back to the drawing board.

Brainstorm your onliness statement with your team. Be playful at first. As you get more serious, you may have an epiphany that inspires you to reframe your brand positioning and differentiation.

If you can't say why your brand is both different and compelling, it's not the statement. Fix your strategy.
Marty Neumeier
ZAG

Today the real competition doesn't come from companies. It comes from clutter.
Marty Neumeier
ZAG

ONLINESS STATEMENT

Our **[product]**   [tablet]

[automobile]

[soft drink]

[furniture]

has the only **[feature]** [operating system]

[tires]

[ingredients]

[materials]

that **[benefit]**   [that never crashes]

[maintains proper pressure]

[has no additives]

[can all be recycled]

Perceptual Mapping

Perceptual mapping is a strategic planning tool that allows the branding team to view your brand in relation to the competition. Used correctly, it helps the branding team decide how to position products and where to enter a new market. The team applies a range of attributes to the mapping process. Typically, the north-south axis is price, and the east-west axis is quality. But it is also productive to plot functional attributes like speed, sustainability, and technological appeal or emotional attributes like passion, trust, or reliability.

Create a series of perceptual maps, plotting attributes that appeal to your customers. Where are the areas of opportunity that you can dominate?

120

You don't have to be great to start, but you have to start to be great.

Zig Ziglar

Strategy and timing are the Himalayas of marketing. Everything else is the Catskills.

Al Ries

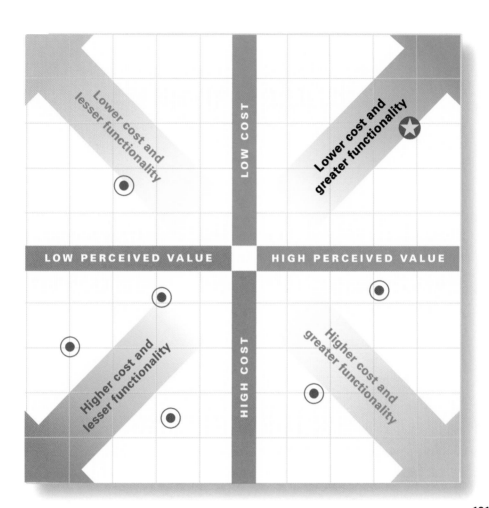

LOW COST

Lower cost and lesser functionality

Lower cost and greater functionality

LOW PERCEIVED VALUE

HIGH PERCEIVED VALUE

HIGH COST

Higher cost and lesser functionality

Higher cost and greater functionality

 Your brand

 Competitors

SWOT Exercise

Strengths Weaknesses Opportunities or Threats, better known as SWOT analysis, is a strategic planning tool. At its best, it can turn threats into opportunities and weaknesses into strengths. The structure of SWOT analysis allows users to identify internal and external forces that can support or undermine an initiative. Strengths and weaknesses are internal characteristics that form an advantage or handicap. Opportunities and threats are external influences that can determine the outcome of the project. A SWOT analysis can illuminate the chance to match a strength to an opportunity or to convert a weakness into a strength.

Honestly assessing internal strengths and weaknesses requires courage and openness. This exercise is most effective when done in a cross-disciplinary group.

You're braver than you believe, stronger than you seem, and smarter than you think.
Christopher Robin

STRENGTHS

WEAKNESSES

OPPORTUNITIES

THREATS

INTERNAL

EXTERNAL

POSITIVE

NEGATIVE

123

Flow

Spontaneous, single-minded absorption in the creative process has been characterized as a sense of flow. Psychologist Mihaly Csíkszentmihályi identified flow as concentrated immersion and complete focus in meeting a challenge. He suggested ways that businesses can set the stage for flow, including:

- Establishing a sense of safety where "all may say what otherwise is only thought."

- Encouraging a bit of craziness.

- Prototyping an idea to try it.

- Seeing differences among participants as an opportunity rather than an obstacle.

To facilitate a sense of flow, set clear goals, where expectations and rules are discernible and goals are attainable.

There are two main strategies we can adopt to improve the quality of life. The first is to try making external conditions match our goals. The second is to change how we experience external conditions to make them fit our goals better.

Mihaly Csikszentmihályi
Flow: The Psychology of Optimal Experience

Time flies. Every action, movement, and thought follows inevitably from the previous one, like playing jazz.

Mihaly Csikszentmihályi
Creativity: Flow and the Psychology of Discovery and Invention

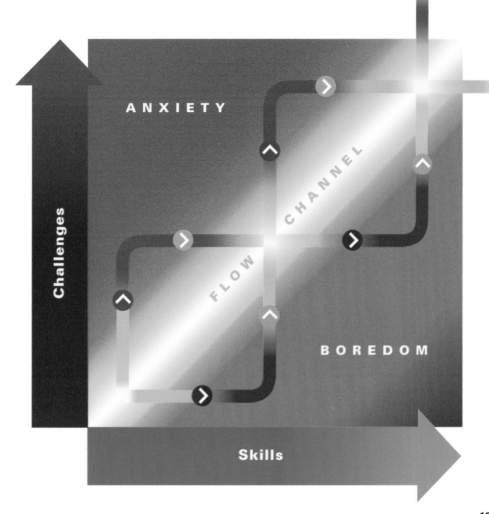

125

Brand Questions   128

Project Management   130

Brand Decisions   131

Branding Process   132

Big Idea Process   133

Bibliography   134

Credits   137

Index   138

Gratitude   141

Authors' Reflections   142

Diagram Matrix   143

Authors   144

126

4
Details

Brand Questions
Use these as conversation starters with your team:

Who are you?

Who needs to know?

Why should they care?

How will they find out?

Why is your brand needed?

If your brand didn't exist, would anyone notice?

What is the purpose of your business aside from making money?

Do you make it easy for your customer to buy?

Do you make it easy for your salesforce to sell?

Do you make it easy for your employees to embrace your brand?

Do your employees understand your vision?

Who are your top three competitors?

How are you different than your top competitors in your industry?

How does your brand demonstrate respect for cultural differences?

What insights do you have into your customer's lifestyle?

Have you embraced the new technologies that your customers are using?

When was the last time you innovated?

How does your brand connect emotionally with your customers?

What platform do you use to communicate with your colleagues in different cities?

Do you have brand guidelines?

How do employees and vendors access your brand guidelines?

Do you have a crisis communications strategy?

Does your organziation have a place for right-brain thinkers?

How collaborative is your culture?

Do you believe that your internal culture is visible to your clients?

How do your employees participate in brand building?

Is your mission statement in a file cabinet or on the wall?

What kinds of experiences do you offer your customers?

What kinds of experiences do your competitors offer customers?

Have you ever conducted an internal brand audit?

Have you ever conducted a competitive audit across marketing channels?

Do you tweet?

Do you have a Facebook page?

Do you blog?

If you covered your logo on your ads, would anyone know it's you?

Have you looked at your website on your digital device?

Have you adjusted your website so that it's legible on a digital device?

When was the last time you created buzz?

How do you listen to what your customers have to say about your brand, product, or service?

Have you ever called your company in the middle of the night and listened to your voicemail?

Have you ever sent an email on your contact page and waited three days for a response?

Do you have email protocol guidelines?

Have you actually tried opening your product packages?

How could you use open source to create a better product or service?

How could you use crowdsourcing to raise money for charity?

How do you build trust with your customers?

Do you have a communications strategy that incorporates social networks?

How does your brand or organization make a difference?

How can your products be more sustainable?

How does your organization measure success?

How transparent are your labor practices?

Do your employees understand compliance issues?

Who's in charge of branding?

Do the people in IT talk to the people in customer service?

When was the last time you conducted an internal message audit?

Should you narrow the focus of your brand?

Should you narrow your offerings or expand them?

When was the last time you delighted a customer?

Project Management Best Practices

Developed by Dr. Ginny Vanderslice, Praxis Consulting Group
Excerpted from *Designing Brand Identity*

Focus

Ability to see and maintain the big picture while also breaking it down into smaller, ordered pieces; ability to keep moving despite challenges and constraints

Discipline

Ability to plan, track numerous tasks, and balance time and cost factors

Strong communication skills

Ability to communicate clearly and respectfully, and to keep team members informed in a timely manner

Empathy

Ability to understand and respond to the needs, viewpoints, and perspectives of all players in the project

Effective management skills

Ability to define needs, priorities, and tasks; ability to make decisions; ability to flag problems; ability to hold people accountable

Adaptability

Ability to stay focused and in control when things go wrong or change in midstream

Creative problem-solving ability

Willingness to see problems as challenges to address rather than as obstacles

Insight

Understanding policies, procedures, corporate culture, key people, and politics

Brand Decisions

Excerpted from *Designing Brand Identity*

Essential characteristics

The CEO leads a small group that includes marketing brand champions.

The entire process is clearly communicated to key stakeholders.

Decisions are aligned with vision and goals.

All members are trusted and respected.

Agreement on goals and positioning strategy precedes creative strategy.

All relevant information and concerns are voiced and tracked.

Pros and cons are always fully discussed.

A commitment is made to communicate about the brand through all levels of the organization.

Focus groups are used as a tool, not as a thought leader.

Decisions are communicated internally first.

Confidentiality is honored.

Critical success factors

The CEO supports this initiative.

The company is ready to invest time, resources, and brainpower.

There is an endpoint that everyone understands and agrees on.

Everyone agrees on how success will be measured.

There is value to the outcome.

Challenging scenarios

The CEO is not involved.

New decision makers get involved in the middle of the process.

Team members' opinions are not respected.

Critical steps in the process are eliminated to save money and time.

Personal aesthetics get confused with functional criteria.

Mergers and acquisitions

Financial stakes are high.

It is difficult to gather input when confidentiality is critical.

The time frame is compressed and atmosphere is tense.

Names and marks are in a symbolic chess match.

Everyone needs the attention of leadership.

It is critical to maintain focus on customer benefit.

Branding Process

Use this process to revitalize a brand or jumpstart a new one.

Phase 1: Conduct Research

Clarify vision, strategies, values, and goals.

Research stakeholders, and customer experience.

Interview management, employees, and partners.

Conduct marketing, competitive, and legal audits.

Evaluate existing brands and brand architecture.

Synthesize insights and present findings.

Phase 2: Clarify Strategy

Clarify brand strategy and brand attributes.

Develop a positioning platform.

Write a brand brief and achieve agreement.

Create key messages.

Write a creative brief for naming and identity.

Phase 3: Design Identity

Visualize the future across touchpoints.

Design brand identity core elements.

Explore experience and look and feel.

Examine brand architecture scenarios.

Present strategy and achieve agreement.

Phase 4: Create Touchpoints

Finalize identity design and system.

Test various scenarios and platforms.

Refine look and feel and messaging.

Initiate trademark protection.

Prioritize and design applications.

Phase 5: Managing Assets

Develop standards and guidelines.

Develop launch strategy and plan.

Launch internally first to employees.

Launch externally to customers and world.

Build synergy; nurture brand champions.

Commit to brand oversight.

Big Idea Process

Use this research process to determine your brand's big idea.

Understand

Vision	Marketing strategy
Values	Competition
Mission	Trends
Value proposition	Pricing
Culture	Distribution
Target market	Research
Segments	Environment
Stakeholder perceptions	Economics
Services	Sociopolitics
Products	Strengths/weaknesses
Infrastructure	Opportunities
	Threats

Clarify

Core values

Brand attributes

Competitive advantage

Brand strategy

Position

Differentiation

Value proposition

Business category

Determine Brand Essence

Central idea

Unifying concept

Key messages

Voice and tone

Big Idea

Brand essence

Bibliography

Aaker, David A. *Managing Brand Equity: Capitalizing on the Value of a Brand Name.* New York: The Free Press, 1991.

Aaker, David A. and Erich Joachimsthaler. *Brand Leadership: The Next Level of the Brand Revolution.* New York: The Free Press, 2000.

Aaker, David A. *Brand Portfolio Strategy: Creating Relevance, Differentiation, Energy, Leverage, and Clarity.* New York: Free Press, 2004.

Adamson, Allen P. *BrandSimple: How the Best Brands Keep It Simple and Succeed.* New York: Palgrave Macmillan, 2006.

Adamson, Allen P. *BrandDigital: Simple Ways Top Brands Succeed in the Digital World.* New York: Palgrave Macmillan, 2008.

Anderson, Chris. *The Long Tail: Why the Future of Business Is Selling Less of More.* New York: Hyperion, 2006.

Anderson, Chris. *Free: The Future of a Radical Price.* New York: Hyperion, 2009.

Bhargava, Rohit. *Personality Not Included: Why Companies Lose Their Authenticity— And How Great Brands Get It Back.* New York: McGraw-Hill, 2008.

Brogan, Chris and Julien Smith. *Trust Agents: Using the Web to Build Influence, Improve Reputation, and Earn Trust.* Hoboken, NJ: John Wiley & Sons, Inc., 2009.

Collins, James C. and Jerry I. Porras. *Built to Last: Successful Habits of Visionary Companies.* New York: HarperCollins, 2002.

Collins, Jim. *Good to Great: Why Some Companies Make the Leap...And Others Don't.* New York: HarperCollins, 2001.

Collins, Jim. *How the Mighty Fall: And Why Some Companies Never Give In.* New York: HarperCollins, 2009.

Covey, Stephen R. *Principle-Centered Leadership.* New York: Fireside, 1992.

Csíkszentmihályi, Mihaly. *Finding Flow: The Psychology of Engagement with Everyday Life.* New York: Basic Books, 1997.

Davis, Scott M. *Brand Asset Management: Driving Profitable Growth Through Your Brands.* San Francisco: John Wiley & Sons, Inc., 2000.

Deal, Terrence E. and Allan A. Kennedy. *Corporate Cultures: The Rites and Rituals of Corporate Life.* New York: Perseus Books Publishing, 2000.

Drucker, Peter F. *Innovation and Entrepreneurship: Practice and Principles.* New York: HarperCollins, 1993.

Dunn, Michael and Chris Halsall. *The Marketing Accountability Imperative: Driving Superior Returns on Marketing Investments.* San Francisco: John Wiley & Sons, Inc., 2009.

Evans, Dave. *Social Media Marketing: An Hour a Day.* Indianapolis: Wiley Publishing, Inc., 2008.

Fried, Jason and David Heinemeier Hansson. *Rework.* New York: Crown Business, 2010.

Friedman, Thomas L. *The World Is Flat: A Brief History of the Twenty-First Century.* New York: Farrar, Straus and Giroux, 2005.

Fung, Victor K., William K. Fung, and Yoram (Jerry) Wind. *Competing in a Flat World: Building Enterprises for a Borderless World.* Upper Saddle River, NJ: Pearson Education, Inc., 2008.

Gladwell, Malcolm. *Blink: The Power of Thinking Without Thinking.* New York: Little, Brown and Company, 2005.

Godin, Seth. *Tribes: We Need You to Lead Us.* New York: Penguin Group, 2008.

Godin, Seth. *Linchpin: Are You Indispensable?* New York: Penguin Group, 2010.

Hartness, Jim and Neil Eskelin. *The 24-Hour Turn-Around.* Grand Rapids, MI: Fleming H. Revell, 1993.

Hawking, Stephen. *The Illustrated Brief History of Time.* New York: Bantam Books, 1996.

Hawking, Stephen. *The Universe in a Nutshell.* New York: Bantam Books, 2001.

Heath, Chip and Dan Heath. *Made to Stick: Why Some Ideas Survive and Others Die.* New York: Random House, 2007.

Heller, Robert and Tim Hindle. *Communicate Clearly.* New York: DK Publishing, Inc., 1998.

Howe, Jeff. *Crowdsourcing: Why the Power of the Crowd Is Driving the Future of Business.* New York: Three Rivers Press, 2009.

Hsieh, Tony. *Delivering Happiness: A Path to Profits, Passion, and Purpose.* New York: Business Plus, 2010.

Kerzner, Harold. *Project Management: A Systems Approach to Planning, Scheduling, and Controlling.* Hoboken, NJ: John Wiley & Sons, Inc., 2009.

Kotler, Philip and Kevin Lane Keller. *Marketing Management.* Upper Saddle River, NJ: Prentice Hall, 2009.

Kuhlmann, Arkadi and Bruce Philp. *The Orange Code: How ING Direct Succeeded by Being a Rebel with a Cause.* Hoboken, NJ: John Wiley & Sons, Inc., 2009.

Laurel, Brenda. *Computers as Theatre.* Boston: Addison-Wesley Longman, 1993.

Lindstrom, Martin. *Brand Sense: Build Powerful Brands through Touch, Taste, Smell, Sight, and Sound.* New York: Free Press, 2005.

Maeda, John. *The Laws of Simplicity: Design, Technology, Business, Life.* London: MIT Press, 2006.

Martin, Patricia. *Tipping the Culture: How Engaging Millennials Will Change Things.* Chicago: LitLamp Communications, 2010. PDF e-book.

Martin, Roger. *The Design of Business: Why Design Thinking Is the Next Competitive Advantage.* Boston: Harvard Business Publishing, 2009.

Mok, Clement. *Designing Business: Multiple Media, Multiple Disciplines.* San Jose, CA: Adobe Press, 1996.

Mollerup, Per. *Brand Book: Branding.* Copenhagen: Børsens Forlag, 2008.

Neumeier, Marty. *The Brand Gap: How to Bridge the Distance between Business Strategy and Design.* Indianapolis: New Riders, 2003.

Neumeier, Marty. *Zag: The Number One Strategy of High-Performance Brands.* Berkeley, CA: New Riders, 2006.

Neumeier, Marty. *The Designful Company: How to Build a Culture of Nonstop Innovation.* Berkeley, CA: New Riders, 2009.

Olins, Wally. *On Brand.* New York: Thames and Hudson, 2004.

Olins, Wally. *The Brand Handbook.* London: Thames and Hudson, 2008.

Peters, Tom. *Re-imagine! Business Excellence in a Disruptive Age.* London: Dorling Kindersley Limited, 2003.

Peters, Tom. *The Little Big Things: 163 Ways to Pursue Excellence*. New York: HarperCollins, 2010.

Phillips, Robbin, Greg Cordell, Geno Church, and Spike Jones. *Brains on Fire: Igniting Powerful, Sustainable, Word of Mouth Movements*. Hoboken, NJ: John Wiley & Sons, Inc., 2010.

Pine, B. Joseph II and James H. Gilmore. *The Experience Economy: Work Is Theatre & Every Business a Stage*. Boston: Harvard Business Publishing, 1999.

Pink, Daniel H. *A Whole New Mind: Why Right-Brainers Will Rule the Future*. New York: Penguin Group, 2009.

Pink, Daniel H. *Drive: The Surprising Truth About What Motivates Us*. New York: Riverhead Books, 2009.

Pinker, Steven. *How the Mind Works*. New York: W.W. Norton & Company, 2009.

President and Fellows of Harvard College. *Harvard Business Review on Brand Management*. Boston: Harvard Business Publishing, 1999.

Reynolds, Garr. *Presentation Zen: Simple Ideas on Presentation Design and Delivery*. Berkeley, CA: New Riders, 2008.

Rhodes, Jerry. *Conceptual Toolmaking: Expert Systems of the Mind*. Cambridge, MA: Blackwell Publishers, 1994.

Ries, Al and Jack Trout. *The 22 Immutable Laws of Marketing: Violate Them at Your Own Risk*. New York: HarperBusiness, 1993.

Ries, Al and Jack Trout. *Positioning: The Battle for Your Mind*. New York: McGraw-Hill, 1994.

Sawhney, Mohanbir. *"Branding in Technology Markets" in Kellogg on Branding: The Marketing Faculty of the Kellogg School of Management*. Alice M. Tybout and Tim Calkins, eds. Hoboken, NJ: John Wiley & Sons, Inc., 2005.

Schmitt, Bernd and Alex Simonson. *Marketing Aesthetics: The Strategic Management of Brands, Identity, and Image*. New York: Free Press, 1997.

Schmitt, Bernd. *Customer Experience Management: A Revolutionary Approach to Connecting with Your Customers*. Hoboken, NJ: John Wiley & Sons, Inc., 2003.

Swaaij, Louise Van, Jean Klare and David Winner. *The Atlas of Experience*. New York: Bloomsbury Publishing, 2000.

Thaler, Linda Kaplan and Robin Koval. *The Power of Nice: How to Conquer the Business World with Kindness*. New York: Doubleday, 2006.

Wind, Yoram (Jerry) and Colin Crook. *The Power of Impossible Thinking: Transform the Business of Your Life and the Life of Your Business*. Upper Saddle River, NJ: Pearson Education, 2005.

Wurman, Richard Saul. *Information Anxiety*. New York: Doubleday, 1989.

Wurman, Richard Saul. *Information Anxiety 2*. Indianapolis: Que, 2001.

Zappos.com. *Zappos.com 2009 Culture Book*. Zappos.com, Inc., 2009.

Credits

Experience diagram, page 29
Adapted with permission from B. Joseph Pine II and James H. Gilmore, *The Experience Economy: Work Is Theatre & Every Business a Stage* (Boston: Harvard Business Publishing, 1999).

Passion diagram, page 31
Inspired by Seth Godin

The Cloud, page 35
Mobility, page 39
Earth image courtesy of NASA

Placemaking diagram, page 45
Adapted with permission from B. Joseph Pine II and James H. Gilmore, Figure 2-2, The Placemaking Portfolio in Full in *Authenticity: What Consumers Really Want* (Boston: Harvard Business Publishing, 2007).

Purpose diagram, page 59
Inspired by Jim Collins's hedgehog concept

Brand Identity Model diagram, page 61
Adapted with permission from David A. Aaker, *Building Strong Brands* (New York: The Free Press, 1996).
Sir Richard Branson photograph reproduced with permission from UPI.
Plane interior photograph by Duane Storey.

Brand as Asset diagram, page 73
Adapted with permission from Marty Neumeier, *The Brand Gap: How to Bridge the Distance between Business Strategy and Design* (Indianapolis: New Riders, 2003).

Brand Extensions diagram, page 75
Adapted with permission from Scott M. Davis, *Brand Asset Management: Driving Profitable Growth Through Your Brands* (San Francisco: John Wiley & Sons, Inc., 2000).

Good and Different diagram, page 87
Adapted with permission from Marty Neumeier, *Zag: The Number One Strategy of High-Performance Brands* (Berkeley, CA: New Riders, 2006).

Culture diagram, page 95
Adapted with permission. © Hanley Brite, Authentic Connections, Inc.

Time Management diagram, page 99
Adapted with permission from Stephen R. Covey, *First Things First.* London: Simon & Schuster, 1994.

Competencies diagram, page 103
Adapted with permission from Michael Dunn and Chris Halsall, *The Marketing Accountability Imperative: Driving Superior Returns on Marketing Investments* (San Francisco: John Wiley & Sons, Inc., 2009).

Insight diagram, page 105
Cloud photograph © Trish Thompson

Customer-centric diagram, page 111
Adapted with permission from Mohanbir Sawhney, "Branding in Technology Markets" in *Kellogg on Branding: The Marketing Faculty of the Kellogg School of Management,* Alice M. Tybout and Tim Calkins, eds. (Hoboken, NJ: John Wiley & Sons, Inc., 2005).

Onliness Exercise diagram, page 119
Adapted with permission from Marty Neumeier, *Zag: The Number One Strategy of High-Performance Brands* (Berkeley, CA: New Riders, 2006).

Flow diagram, page 125
Adapted with permission from Mihaly Csíkszentmihályi, *Finding Flow: The Psychology of Engagement with Everyday Life.* New York: Basic Books, 1997.

Authors' portraits, page 144
© Ed Wheeler

Index

A

Aaker, David, 60
Adamson, Allen P., 92
Adobe, 80, 81
A Hundred Monkeys, 84
Altman, Danny, 84
American Girl Place, 28
Anderson, Chris, 42
Apple, 74, 85
Apple Store, 44
Apps, 38
Audit, 56
Authenticity, 64
Authentic Connections, 94
Avarde, Susan, 90

B

Bayn, 82, 83
B Corporations, 68
Bennis, Warren, 30
Birdsall, Connie, 100
Big idea, 70
Big idea process, 133
Birdsall, Connie, 62
Bitetto, James, 84
Bloomberg Businessweek, 38
Brains on Fire, 18, 70
Brand alignment, 76
Brand architecture, 78
Brand as asset, 72
Brand as identity, 50
Brand basics, 48–87
Brand decision making, 131
Brand extensions, 74
Brand Finance PLC, 72

Brand identity planning model, 60
Branding, 90
Branding process, 90, 132
Brand landscape, 10–47
Brand management, 88–125
Brand questions, 128–129
Branson, Richard, 60
Brin, Sergey, 86
Brite, Hanley, 94
Brogan, Chris, 20, 26, 68
Budweiser, 80
Buffet, Warren, 32

C

Caldwell, Heidi, 114
Calista, Dan, 116
Carbone, Ken, 76
Carbone Smolan, 76
Chase, Robin, 16
Choice, 46
Citi, 90
Cloud, 34
Cloud computing, 34
Coca-Cola, 72
Cody, Heidi, 80
Collaboration, 96
Collins, Jim, 58
Comet Skateboards, 12
Competencies, 102
Conversation, 20
Covey, Stephen, 98
Creativity, 16,124
Cronan, 104
Cronan, Michael, 104
Crosby, Bart, 90
Crosby Associates, 90
Crowdsourcing, 40
Csíkszentmihályi, Mihaly, 124

Cullen, Moira, 82, 96
Culture, 94
Customer-centric, 110
Customer service, 108

D

Dave Matthews Band, 50
Davis, Scott M., 50, 74
De La Garza, Sam, 20
Design thinking, 16
Desire, 54
Deutsch, Blake, 14, 56, 80, 98, 100, 102, 114, 116
Disney, 80, 81
Donovan/Green, 28
Drive, 88–125
Droid, 38, 46
Drucker, Peter, 102
Dunn, Michael, 102, 112
Dynamics, 10–47

E

eBay, 52
Edelman, Richard, 106
Edelman Worldwide, 106
Einstein, Albert, 104
Epictetus, 114
Experience, 28

F

Facebook, 18, 26, 32
Fight or flight, 116
Flickr, 85
Flow, 124
Focus, 106
Ford Fiesta, 20
Footprint Chronicles, 12
Forrester Research, 38
Free, 42
Freeconomics, 42
Fring app, 42

G

GE, 70

Galuppo, Gail, 56

Geek Squad, 28

Gilbert, Jay Coen, 68

Gilmore, James H., 28, 44, 64, 110

Glaser, Milton, 80

Glee, 86

Global sourcing, 12

Godin, Seth, 30, 64

Good and different, 86

Google, 42, 52, 83, 86

Gorman, Margie, 26

Grams, Chris, 40, 66

Green, Nancye, 28

Gregerman, Alan, 96

Growth, 112

H

Hedgehog model, 58

Herman Miller, 70, 85

Hershey, 82, 96

Hierarchy of needs, 54

Hogan, Michel, 76

Hollis, Nigel, 22

Howe, Jeff, 40

Hsieh, Tony, 94

Hulu, 86

Human Business Works, 20

I

IBM, 34, 38, 70, 85

IBM Smarter Planet, 34

IDEO, 92

Immelt, Jeff, 70

Innovation, 16

Insight, 104

Intelligence, 48–87

Interconnected, 22

iPad, 38, 44, 46, 86

iPhone, 22, 38, 46, 76

Iyengar, Sheena, S. 46

J

Jacobs, Bert, 36, 52

Jensen, Cheryl, 12

Jobs, Steve, 74

Jooste, Genevieve, 14

K

Kedrosky, Paul, 38

Kelley, Tom, 92

Koch, Richard, 100

Kotler, Philip, 54

L

Left brain, right brain, 17

LEGO, 44

Legoland, 44

Life is good, 36, 52

Linux, 24

Lippincott, 20, 62, 100

Liquid Agency, 86

Logos, 82

Long-term brand equity, 113

Lux, Elizabeth, 68

M

Management Innovation eXchange, 30

Marketing competencies, 102

Martin, Patricia, 40

Martin, Roger, 16

Maslow, Abraham, 54

Matthews, Dave, 50

Mau, Bruce, 30

Metrics, 114

Merriam-Webster, 94

Miller, Abbott, 56

Millward Brown, 72

MIX, 30

Mobility, 38

Moore, Gordon, 14

Moore's Law, 14

Murphy, Brendán, 20

N

Names, 84

  Acronym, 85

  Descriptive, 85

  Fabricated, 85

  Founder, 85

  Magic spell, 85

  Metaphor, 85

Naming, 84

Needs and desire, 54

Netflix, 80, 81

Neumeier, Marty, 16, 72, 86, 118

New Kind, 40, 66, 106

Nike, 82, 83

Nissan, 12

O

Olins, Wally, 62, 78

Onliness exercise, 118

Open source, 24

Opensource.com, 24

Opp, Jonathan, 106

Oxfam, 52

P

Pareto Principle, 100
Passion, 30
Patagonia, 12
Pausch, Randy, 98
Pentagram, 56, 90
Perception, 62
Perceptual mapping, 120
Peters, Tom, 74, 92
Phillips, Robbin, 70
Pine, B. Joseph II, 28, 44, 46, 64, 110
Pink, Daniel, 16, 24
Placemaking, 44
Porter, Michael, 36
Positioning, 66
Praxis Consulting Group, 116
Project management best practices, 130
Prophet, 60, 102, 112
Purpose, 58

R

Radiohead, 42
Recognition, 80
Red Hat, 24
Reese's, 80
Ries, Al, 66, 120
Robin, Christopher, 122
Romer, Paul, 14

S

Sawhney, Mohanbir, 110
Scher, Paula, 90
Schultz, Howard, 82
Sen, Shubhro, 12

Shea, Gregory P., 22
Short-term revenue generation, 113
Simplicity, 92
Smartphone, 38, 62
Smith, Julien, 26, 68
Social entrepreneurs, 30, 36
Social networks, 20, 26
Sorrell, Martin, 92
Speed, 14
Spirit and soul, 60
Stakeholders, 68
Starbucks, 82, 83
Sterling Brands, 66
Strengths, weaknesses, opportunities, and threats (SWOT), 122
Sustainability, 36
SWOT analysis, 122

T

Thompson, Clive, 32
Time management, 98
TiVo, 85
TOMS Shoes, 36
Touchpoints, 56
Trademarks, 82, 83, 85
   Abstract/symbolic mark, 83
   Emblem, 83
   Letterform, 83
   Pictorial mark, 83
   Wordmark, 83
Transparency, 32, 68
Tribes, 30
Triple bottom line, 36
Trout, Jack, 66
Twitter, 86, 92

U

Unilever, 70
Univision, 82, 83

V

Vanderslice, Ginny, 116, 130
Venture Works, 96
Virgin, 60, 61
Vision, 52
Volvo, 118
Vynamic, 116

W

Wales, Jimmy, 58
Walker, Brian, 70
Western Union, 56
Whirlwind, 36
White, Tyler, 22
Whitehurst, Jim, 24
Wikipedia, 58
Wittenstein, Mike, 110
Word of mouth, 18, 32

Y

YouTube, 85

Z

Zappos, 94, 108
Zappos Family Core Values, 108
Ziglar, Zig, 120
Zipcar, 16
Zuckerberg, Mark, 32

Gratitude

In our long and fulfilling careers, we have been privileged to collaborate with a great many people—colleagues, mentors, clients, business partners, employees, teachers, interns, and students. We learned from all of them, and all of them enriched and shaped our professional and personal life. Our interaction and relationships with them are responsible for who and where we are today. You know who you are.

Our families have been a source of inspiration and strength during our careers and this project. We are fortunate to both have spouses who believe in the our work and this book, and who are supportive, insightful, and intellectually rigorous: Alina's husband Ed Wheeler and their daughters, Tessa Wheeler and Tearson Morrison; Joel's wife Trish Thompson and their son, Ben Katz.

Our team

Alina Wheeler's team: Lissa Reidel, collaborator, whose insights and skills contributed to *Brand Atlas* content. Megan Stanger, assitant, whose positive attitude and organizational skills kept the brand lab vital to this process.

Joel Katz Design Associates interns Ari Winkleman and Charles Wybierala, who constructed many of the diagrams with expertise and sensitivity.

Our publisher

Our editor Margaret Cummins and our publisher John Wiley & Sons for their relentless commitment to excellence. Our Wiley team:

Amanda Miller, VP and publisher

Justin Mayhew, associate marketing director

Penny Makras, marketing manager

Diana Cisek, production director

Lauren Poplawski, editorial program coordinator

Victor Aranjo, senior copywriter

Deirdre Silver, legal director

Dani Pumilla, contracts analyst

David Riedy, art director

Hillary Fogel, project supervisor

Gretchen Dykstra, proofreader.

Our colleagues

Perpetual gratitude for open, honest, thought-provoking conversations with Jon Bjornson, Steve Frykholm, Dan Calista, Karin Hibma, Michael Cronan, Marty Neumeier, Ashis Bhattacharya, Andy Lamas, Dan Dimmock, Jim Gilmore, Joe Pine, Max Ritz, Sylvia Harris, LeRoux Jooste, Hilary Jay, Craig Johnson, and Dustin Britt.

141

Authors' Reflections

Brand Atlas was created from a mutual desire to rethink and reimagine a brand resource for a world overwhelmed with information. What if we distilled a vast amount of brand thinking, and provided just enough content to scan and spark meaningful conversations? What if we used provocative diagrams to illuminate concepts, processes, and tools? What if we reversed the relationship between expansive text and minimal diagrams and created a business book that appealed to visual learners?

Brand Atlas is designed for a new genera-tion of brand builders. Why another book on branding when the existing thought leadership is extensive and intelligent? We believe that it is time for a radically different resource that synthesizes and visualizes marketplace dynamics, fun-damental brand concepts, and brand management tools and processes. We wanted to appeal to the reader who has little time but great desire to understand brand fundamentals quickly. We wanted to consider the reader's experience, from the printed page to the tablet to the smart-phone.

Distilling content and designing fifty-three diagrams has been a daunting and rewarding process. Data visualization is omnipresent and frequently software generated. We wanted to create original diagrams that visualized ideas and con-cepts rather than data. Technology has become so provocative and powerful that it often distracts us from the most mean-ingful work ahead of us: to be original, to think about big ideas, and to design a better future.

Simplicity, clarity, consistency, and the avoidance of confusing, misleading, and superfluous data are paramount to diagram design. We could fill an entire book with our beliefs about what makes a successful diagram. (That, however, is Joel's next project.) In *Brand Atlas,* diagrams exist to advance understanding, simplify complex dynamics, illustrate how things work, and illuminate the relationship of parts to each other and to the whole. The challenge was to realize a simple, bold, and coherent visual language without predictability or redundancy.

Brand Atlas was a dream collaboration. Our history with each other spans over 30 years. Between 1980 and 1992, we were the principals of Katz Wheeler Design. The strength of our work, both past and present, is based on an unswerving com-mitment to doing whatever it takes to make it right. We are different people today except in our definition of excel-lence. This has been a challenging project: brevity is hard.

The collaboration took place in numerous locations, mostly in Philadelphia, but Joel worked from Paris and Rome for months in 2009 and 2010. When possible, Alina worked at Skylight, her mountain home in the Adirondacks.

As we look back on a long and arduous process, would we do it again? Absolutely: we thrive on challenge. The reward has been the collaborative process and the product itself. We look forward to feedback from our readers and colleagues, confident that the conversation will be robust.

Alina Wheeler
Joel Katz

About the Authors

For comments about this book, email
authors@brandatlas.info

Alina Wheeler is a branding consultant and author of *Designing Brand Identity: An Essential Guide for the Whole Branding Team* (Wiley), the best selling global resource for businesses and nonprofits. She works with leaders to accelerate brand clarity and awareness. Her disciplined process has been used successfully by large, complex organizations like Vanguard, and nonprofit organizations like Thomas Jefferson's Poplar Forest. Alina frequently speaks to management teams, practitioners, and students around the world. She is a former national board member of AIGA and a member of the Identity Works Forum. She is married to Ed Wheeler, a photographer. They have two daughters and two grandsons.

www.alinawheeler.com
For consulting engagements and speaking inquiries
alina@alinawheeler.com

Joel Katz is an internationally known information designer and authority on the visualization of complex information. A Fellow of the American Academy in Rome and AIGA Philadelphia, he lectures widely and teaches information design at The University of the Arts and Philadelphia University. Katz holds a BA Scholar of the House with Exceptional Distinction from Yale College, where he won the Strong Prize in American Literature, and BFA and MFA degrees in graphic design from the Yale School of Art. His design is in the collections of the Cooper-Hewitt Museum and the Museums of Modern Art, New York, Tokyo, and Kyoto. His photography has been exhibited in the U.S. and Europe. He is currently writing a book on information design. Joel Katz is married to Trish Thompson, an artist; they have one son.

www.joelkatzdesign.com
www.joelkatzphotography.com
For design consulting and speaking inquiries
jkatz@joelkatzdesign.com